FEASTING ON HOPE

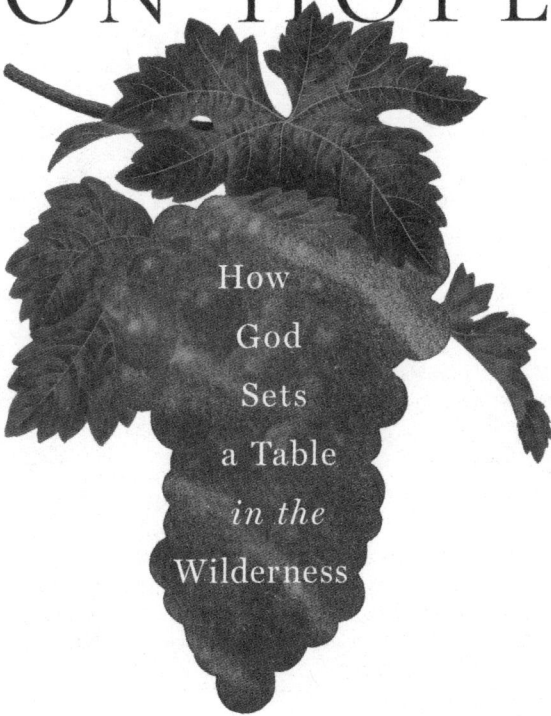

How
God
Sets
a Table
in the
Wilderness

HANNAH MILLER KING

Foreword by Esau McCaulley

ivp

An imprint of InterVarsity Press
Downers Grove, Illinois

InterVarsity Press
P.O. Box 1400 | Downers Grove, IL 60515-1426
ivpress.com | email@ivpress.com

InterVarsity Press® is the publishing division of InterVarsity Christian Fellowship/USA®. For more information, visit intervarsity.org.

Scripture quotations, unless otherwise noted, are from The Holy Bible, English Standard Version. ESV© Text Edition: 2016. Copyright © 2001 by Crossway Bibles, a publishing ministry of Good News Publishers. Used by permission. All rights reserved.

While any stories in this book are true, some names and identifying information may have been changed to protect the privacy of individuals.

The publisher cannot verify the accuracy or functionality of website URLs used in this book beyond the date of publication.

Cover design: Faceout Studio, Spencer Fuller
Interior design: Jeanna Wiggins
Images: © Joanna McCarthy / The Image Library via Getty Images

ISBN 978-1-5140-1114-0 (print) | ISBN 978-1-5140-1115-7 (digital)

Printed in the United States of America ∞

Library of Congress Cataloging-in-Publication Data
A catalog record for this book is available from the Library of Congress.

32   31   30   29   28   27   26 | 13   12   11   10   9   8   7   6   5   4   3   2   1

FOR MY SIBLINGS,

in thanksgiving for the table

we shared growing up.

AND FOR MY CHILDREN,

in hope that you will always know home

at our family table and at his.

CONTENTS

FOREWORD

Esau McCaulley

THERE IS A DANGER IN FOREWORDS. It can be like someone coming on stage before the comedian and explaining all the jokes that the audience is about to hear. It can be similar to a guide at an art exhibit pointing out all the details in a painting that is best simply taken in. The best response to poetry is often silent reflection, not exposition.

I will try to avoid all those things because Hannah Miller King's excellent book deserves better. *Feasting on Hope* is part memoir, part reflection on the beauty of Communion (the Eucharist), part theodicy, and so much more besides. More than anything else, it is a profoundly moving God-honoring work that travels the difficult road through pain to beauty. *Feasting on Hope* is consistently mystical but always grounded, earthy, and yet transcendent.

As a pastor, this will be the book I give to people looking for an introduction to the sacramental life. I am confident that others will do the same. I would say more, but any description that I might give will pale in comparison to your experience of the thing itself.

A TALE OF TWO TABLES

SOME OF MY EARLIEST MEMORIES take place at the dinner table.

Ours was in a sunroom with floor-to-ceiling windows that gave the effect of eating outside. When I got antsy in my seat, I would crane my neck to see the tops of trees and what they might drop onto our skylights. Sometimes pine needles would build up in the windowpanes until the wind blew them free.

Usually, though, there was plenty to observe around the table. As the second oldest of six children, I was rarely bored at mealtimes. To my eyes, our eight-foot-long table was about as big as a swimming pool. It was also usually crowded, noisy, and entertaining. Sometimes special guests or grandparents would be brave enough to join us for a meal, and we'd encounter new stories or menu items.

One particularly social evening—probably a holiday, when food and people filled every square inch of space, and all the special dishes were out—I thought I might take advantage of the crowd and slip under the table undetected. My plan was to sneak past the rows of adult feet to the end of the table where the butter dish lay, unattended and enticing. I reached up for it, took a large bite out of the middle of the soft yellow stuff I always wanted more of, then slid it back onto the table above my head. I thought it was the perfect heist; nobody could possibly suspect me. When I climbed back up into my seat, every adult in the room was grinning in my direction.

When I reflect on how I felt after getting caught in my first act of theft, I remember incredulity. How did they all know? I also remember disappointment. Apparently, butter tastes much better on bread. But I do not remember shame. There was a safety in that first community around the table, a permission to become myself through trial and error and the input of wise guides. I wasn't perfect or the center of things, but I belonged. In my early years, I enjoyed the kind of stability that children can intuit even if they can't articulate.

The stability was short-lived.

After a series of cross-country moves, we were living in a temporary home—with plans to build my parents' dream house nearby—when my father was diagnosed with an aggressive form of cancer. For the next four years, our family life was in constant flux. We moved again, but not into the dream house. We changed schools three times.

My parents made every effort to save my father's life, which required a fair amount of travel. While they pursued experimental medical treatments at top hospitals, my siblings and I were split up and sent to various other homes. We stayed with friends and relatives who could keep us for three or four weeks at a time.

My first extended stay away from my parents was over Thanksgiving. I was eleven. For the most part, I had a great time playing with my cousins and hearing my aunt tell stories from when my dad was a kid. On this trip I learned to shuffle a deck of cards and use the (dial-up) internet on the family computer in their kitchen. But it was also when the insomnia began. At night, I was haunted by an aching sadness I couldn't explain or understand. I just knew I wasn't home and that nothing was the same as it was before. At the borrowed tables of friends and relatives, I was always a partial outsider.

My father died slowly. This was a gift because it meant we got more time, more memories with him. But it was also a curse because as he declined, those memories grew more tragic. One winter, my younger brother and I were in our school's production of *A Christmas Carol*. My dad insisted on coming to see it. We set up an armchair in the auditorium for him to attend comfortably, but during the performance he began seizing and had to be carried outside by four other men.

After he died, the bank foreclosed on our home and we moved again, into an old parsonage behind a Lutheran church that gave my mom a good deal on rent. Either because it was a smaller space than we'd ever lived in, or because my mother couldn't bear to look at my father's empty chair every day, she shoved our massive dining table against a window in the new dining room. It now only seated seven.

Childhood loss interrupted my sense of safety and belonging in the world. Ordinary transitions, like a move to a different house or visits with cousins, were colored by traumatic transitions—like death. The result was a cumulative feeling of homelessness, a displacement and disconnection in the presence of others. Subconsciously, I internalized this vulnerability as shame.

This was the subtext of my story when I began taking weekly Communion at my church.

I was halfway through seminary by then and had already experienced a fair amount of healing. Committed mentors, skilled therapists, and a praying mother had helped to preserve my Christian faith and nourish my burgeoning call to ministry. But when I began worshiping at a church that invited me to walk to the front each week with empty hands outstretched, to look another human being in the eye in hopes of being fed, all my childhood insecurity rose straight to the surface.

Every week, I struggled to come forward and receive Communion. But at the end of each service, we prayed a prayer that interpreted my tears. In unison, the congregation said:

Almighty God, eternal Father,
we have sat at your feet,
learned from your word,
and eaten from your table.
We give you thanks and praise
for accepting us into your family.
Send us out with your blessing,
to live and to witness for you in the power of your Spirit,
through Jesus Christ, the firstborn from the dead.[1]

In the practice of Communion, I was invited to rehearse bodily what I believed doctrinally: By grace, we are grafted into God's family. I knew this intellectually, but was undone by the tangible, liturgical expression of Christ's profound welcome. Week after week as I came to the Table—his Table—he confronted my fear of abandonment, my feelings of displacement, my shame. And in exchange he offered me himself. Slowly, I found a new sense of belonging at this Table.

The Bible describes Christian faith primarily in familial terms. Those who follow Jesus are called his bride, his body, his brothers and sisters. In teaching his disciples to pray, he instructed us to call God "Father."[2] And in teaching us to worship, he instituted a meal. In my tradition we call this meal a "sacrament," which stems from the word *mystery*: When we share the Lord's Supper, we mysteriously experience fellowship with him. We eat from his table. We are accepted into his family.

Belonging to God's family doesn't replace our family of origin. It doesn't erase traumatic memories or the ache of personal losses. But it does write them into a larger story of hope. Communion with Christ reorients us to face our various griefs from a place of safety and strength. In him we find a home.

I've been receiving weekly Communion for about twelve years now. As a priest, I am often on the other side of the Table from where I first began receiving. When I hold the bread and wine before my congregation, I extend to them the same invitation that healed me: "Taste and see that the Lord is good!"[3] I do so even though my own healing isn't complete—and won't be until he comes.

Despite what many of us have been taught, either overtly or through the power of suggestion, Christianity does not promise total renewal in this life.

In his letter to the Romans, the apostle Paul describes the Christian experience as a kind of groaning; we eagerly await our full redemption because we know it hasn't arrived yet. Our salvation is secure, but we haven't yet reaped all its benefits. He elaborates, "For in this hope we were saved. Now hope that is seen is not hope. For who hopes for what he already sees? But if we hope for what we do not see, we wait for it with patience."[4]

I used to think that if I could just learn to trust God enough, the shadow of childhood loss would lift entirely. I assumed that any remaining unfulfilled longing inside me reflected my deficient faith. But at the Lord's Table, my grief has been both healed and stoked. In celebrating a meal that anticipates Christ's return, we aren't meant to be fully satisfied now. Christian hope is future-oriented:

it trains us to fix our eyes on the horizon, expectant for the day to dawn that will make all things new. Until then, Paul says, we see as in a mirror. But on that day, we will see face to face. We will know fully, just as we have been fully known.[5]

My family table remains incomplete in the face of permanent loss. Christian faith does not change that. Jesus never promised to protect us from living with unmet longings or unresolved pain. But he has promised to be with us until the end of this age. And he has provided everything we need to sustain us while we wait. He has prepared a table for us.[6]

In Psalm 78, God's people are instructed to remember and trust his sustaining presence. The psalmist retells the story of their exodus from slavery and of God's faithfulness in their long journey through the desert. Despite God's miraculous provision, his people still doubted. After he'd parted the sea, made water gush from a rock, and led them by a pillar of fire, they questioned his character and his competence by asking, "Can God spread a table in the wilderness?"

I understand their question. In the presence of enduring grief and unfulfilled desires, it's easy to feel anxious. As we anticipate the full, unbroken fellowship that awaits, we are tempted to ask, "Can God spread a table in the wilderness?" This book is my own psalm of response: yes, he can. He already has.

1

HOPE

The Feast and the Foretaste

---

*What you believe about the future will
change how you live in the present.*

DANIEL NAYERI, *EVERYTHING SAD IS UNTRUE*

I WAS ELEVEN when my father was diagnosed with terminal cancer.

He and my mom came home from the doctor one morning after what I assumed was a routine check-up—if he'd been having symptoms of some unseen illness, I didn't know it—and they corralled us all into their bedroom to "talk." This was unusual, but my dad often had a grandiose way about him, so we complied without too much confusion.

Their bedroom wasn't large. I'm not sure why they chose to crowd six children into this space for our life-altering conversation. Maybe it was the place in our house with fewest distractions. No toys, no snacks in eyesight. Maybe their room represented their own safe place. Its central feature was two large windows on the far side of the bed that bathed the ancient wood floors in sunlight.

That's what I remember most from our conversation. Not the words exchanged, not my siblings' reactions to the news; just the shimmering white light pouring over my dad's enormous frame as he spoke.

He said, "Today we found out that Daddy has cancer. And we have decided that whether I live or die, we want my life to glorify God."

In the years since this moment, I've wrestled with how to articulate its impact on me. I don't believe that God glibly kills people—that he removes fathers, mothers, friends, spouses—to teach us a lesson or to "get glory." I also know that my father didn't just accept his cancer diagnosis like a death sentence. During the four years of his illness he fought, literally, for dear life.

But the words he spoke over us at the beginning of this journey were like a prophecy: They invited me into a truth I will never fully understand. They introduced me to the mystery that a life yielded to God is a glorious life, regardless of outcomes.

This mystery does not fit neatly into our paradigms.

Religious or not, we all have a script in mind for the story of our lives. We expect, or at least we hope, that circumstances will work out in our favor. Some struggle is permissible as long as there's a happy ending. My young sons, who've been catechized by Disney and other kid-friendly films, reassure each other during tense moments on family movie night: "The good guys are going to win." But what happens when they don't? How do we find equilibrium when our personal narratives take an unexpected turn and deprive us of the resolution we crave?

These questions are especially troubling for Christians, who believe in a God that is both powerful and good. When God allows tragedies to occur, people of faith are rightly scandalized. Our oldest prayer book, the Psalms, is full of the question *why*? Sometimes, it is the only honest word of faith we can muster.

Early in my father's battle with cancer, we anticipated healing. Confident in God's abilities, we prayed for a miracle. But after four years of praying and hoping and submitting to every treatment available—including, to our shared dismay, gallons of fresh carrot juice and other dietary changes that we implemented as a family— the miracle never came. My father died at age forty-four. Twenty years later, I'm still asking *why*? It's a question I've learned to carry with me, like a piece of jewelry I never take off. It's simply there, so much a part of me that I rarely notice it anymore. But this unanswerable question has also become like an expansive room in which I live, and where I have met God more profoundly than if our prayers had been answered as we hoped.

In the bewilderment of grief, we come to the end of ourselves and our paradigms. We encounter a reality beyond our ability to control. In the wilderness of *why*, we come face to face with God. Perhaps, when my father was diagnosed, he recognized this: that even when God can't be understood, he can be trusted.

Crisis disrupted my script. But paradoxically, it gave me a better one.

Christian hope is often articulated in seemingly oppositional ways. Either we have an imagination for healing and renewal in this life, or we teach patience in suffering while we wait for heaven. Sometimes we fluctuate between these two frameworks. My family's own journey reflects this.

During my father's illness, we worshiped for a season with Christians who confidently prayed for his cancer to be reversed. We were energized by their joyful expectation that God, who raised

Jesus from the dead, is still at work in the world. But when my
father wasn't healed, I struggled to pick up the pieces of our faith.
Things hadn't gone according to the formula. In the wake of his
death, my theological maxims came to a breaking point: Was this
tragedy my fault or God's? Had my faith not been strong enough,
or had God not been true to his word?

We needed a bigger frame for our grief.

As a struggling teenager, I was comforted to learn about God's
mysterious reign over all circumstances, even the bad ones. I
needed to hear that his good plan does not ultimately rest on the
strength of my faith, and that no loss is outside of his power or his
mercy. But at times I wondered how to reconcile this newfound
understanding of God's sovereignty with my former expectation
that he acts powerfully on behalf of our prayers.

In the face of a cancer diagnosis—or chronic illness or job loss
or divorce papers—we scramble to make meaning and find a way
forward. And the Christian story offers a spectrum of possibilities:
Do we continue to "ask, seek, and knock" for what we believe God
can accomplish by his power?[1] Or should we entrust our circumstances to the One who works all things according to the counsel
of his will?[2] The answer, of course, is both. Full-throated Christian
hope cultivates an imagination for present renewal alongside a theology of suffering. But holding these things in tension takes practice.
And it takes *practices*.

The earliest Christian ritual is an exercise in hope.

The Lord's Supper began, appropriately, with the Lord himself.
On the night before he died, Jesus reinterpreted the Jewish Passover
meal in light of his own ministry. For centuries, God's people had
celebrated their deliverance from Egypt by sharing a meal that allowed them to remember—and, with the senses, to reenact—the

historic night that God secured their freedom. In associating the elements of this meal with himself, Jesus claimed them as symbols of a "new covenant," a new promise of deliverance for those who'd follow him in faith. He also promised that one day, he would share table fellowship with them again in person.[3] Among his first followers, then, the Lord's Supper was equal parts remembrance and longing: They celebrated Jesus' victory over sin and death, and they looked eagerly for his return. This poignant meal was a centerpiece of their worship from the earliest days of the church.[4]

In the first century, Christians gathered for worship under threat of persecution. Both Jewish and Roman leaders deemed allegiance to Christ problematic and sought to snuff it out through violence. The apostle Paul, himself the recipient of extreme persecution, addressed the reality of suffering in almost all his letters to churches.

Peter, who would eventually die by crucifixion, encouraged other believers to see their hardship as both normative and lasting: stand "firm in your faith, knowing that the same kinds of suffering are being experienced by your brotherhood throughout the world."[5] For the first Christians, patience in suffering was nonnegotiable. Jesus' own words were still fresh in their collective memory: "In the world you will have trouble."[6]

But the early church also believed and acted in accordance with the second half of Jesus' promise about trouble. On his last night with the disciples he'd said, "In the world you will have trouble. *But take heart; I have overcome the world.*" In this hope, Jesus' followers gathered to break bread at the risk of their own lives.

On the first Easter morning, God demonstrated that his victory over sin and death is both secure and has already broken into the present age in the body of Jesus. His resurrection was proof that renewal is real, and it has arrived. The bread and wine, then, which Jesus described as his own body and blood, became a sample of the new world that is coming. The Lord's Supper is a taste of resurrection—of new creation—here and now. This meal literally feeds our imaginations for what is possible in Christ, even as it reminds us of all that remains incomplete until we see him face to face. The central practice of Christian worship helps us hold seemingly opposite versions of hope in tension. At Jesus' table, we feast on the life that conquered death— and we proclaim that death until he returns to complete his work.

This tension is characteristic of the time in which we live: Jesus has been raised from the dead, but he has not yet returned to make all things new. Theologians often call this time-between-the times "the already-not-yet," in which God's Kingdom has *already* been inaugurated on earth but is *not yet* fully established.[7] As those who follow Jesus in this overlap of ages, we can and should expect to see evidence of his Kingdom among us in many forms, from physical healing to spiritual transformation to social renewal. But we should also expect that some things will remain unhealed until the King returns to finish what he started.

Living with tension is hard work. Despite our best efforts to create one, there's no algorithm or formula by which we can predict exactly when or how God's Kingdom will manifest itself here and now. Sometimes, prayers are answered beyond our imagining. Sometimes they are not. This mystery compels some of us to try harder to "crack the code" of God's power, to search desperately for an explanation or a principle by which we can obtain our desired outcomes. Others of us, fearing the discouragement or disillusionment that may accompany unanswered prayers, decide to stop praying for a desired outcome altogether. We would rather not ask than risk being disappointed.

Beginning in high school, I developed chronic back pain that progressed into my early twenties. I visited an array of doctors and tried numerous treatments, exercise regimens, and dietary tweaks.

Nothing brought lasting relief. My aches and pains were well known by my church friends and prayer groups. "How's your back today?" they'd politely ask as I fidgeted in my chair or stood up to stretch awkwardly in the corner.

"About the same," I'd respond.

By halfway through seminary, the pain was so intense that I was often in tears by early evening. One Sunday in December, I was sitting (uncomfortably, as usual) in church when I felt prompted to ask someone to pray for my healing. But the thought of asking again, and hearing *no* again, seemed almost unbearable. I didn't know if I could handle the rejection. When I finally did muster up the courage to ask a volunteer to pray for me, I downplayed my request. "Please pray for my back," was all I could say.

To my surprise, I was healed that morning.

Twelve years and three children later, the chronic pain has not returned. I do not know why my prayers were answered that day and not in the years leading up to it. I do not know why my father's prayers for healing remained unanswered despite our many fervent requests. These experiences don't add up in a neat, mathematical equation. They illustrate the tension of our time: the "already-not-yet" of God's Kingdom on earth.

When I come to the Lord's Table on a Sunday morning, I do not regret asking for my father's healing. The bread in my hands validates my childhood faith, reminding me that in raising Jesus from the dead, God has already done the impossible. We should feel no shame in asking for miracles, seeking family reconciliation, or working for justice in the world. As Esau McCaulley put it, Jesus' resurrection "reshapes the Christian imagination, forever obliterating the limits we place upon our Creator."[8]

If I didn't have the repetitive practice of Communion to keep this truth in front of me, the sting of unanswered prayers might be enough to dampen my hope. But at the Table, my unanswered prayers find a place as well. They are caught up into the collective longing of the church throughout history that prays, "Come quickly, Lord Jesus." Our experiences of persistent grief help us get in touch with the fact that right now, we feast in Jesus' absence. We celebrate the start of new creation, but we still live with the shadow of death until he returns to wipe every tear from our eyes.

Whether we gather for worship under the threat of persecution, in the fresh wake of a national tragedy, or in the quiet pain of personal loss, we gather as those with visceral awareness that the story of redemption isn't over yet. Our present pain teaches us to yearn more sincerely for the day when Jesus will set things right. In this way, unmet longings don't hinder our faith, they enhance it. They release us from the pressure to look or feel as if we've "arrived" at complete wholeness, and they increase our desire for the sustenance God has provided in the meantime.

In a world obsessed with eradicating discomfort, the Lord's Supper is prophetic. At the Table, we name the hunger that cannot be fully satiated here and now. The meal that feeds us is both a feast and a foretaste. When it's presented as a version of the American dream, in which prosperity can be achieved through adherence to certain maxims, Christianity falls flat. There are better ways to get rich or stay healthy.

But when our faith sustains hope *despite* short-term disillusionment, we learn a way of being-in-the-world that is rooted in the next one. "The world to come," as the Nicene Creed describes it, is the world we humans are looking for. We won't create it through human collaboration or the right politics. We can't protect our personal versions of it from tragedy or loss. And even when we try, we can't entirely snuff out our God-given belief that it exists and is our home. C. S. Lewis calls it our "inconsolable secret," this desire for a "far-off country" that haunts the religious and nonreligious alike:

> I am trying to rip open the inconsolable secret in each one of you—the secret which hurts so much that you take your revenge on it by calling it names like Nostalgia and Romanticism and Adolescence. . . . Our commonest expedient is to call it beauty and behave as if that had settled the matter. . . . These things—the beauty, the memory of our own past—are good images of what we really desire; but if they are mistaken for the thing itself they turn into dumb idols, breaking the hearts of their worshipers. For they are not the thing itself; they are only the scent of a flower we have not found, the echo of a tune we have not heard, news from a country we have never yet visited.[9]

At the Lord's Supper, we taste the food from that far-off country. We bear witness to the fact that there is another world, in which the dead are raised and the impaired fellowship of humanity is restored. Right now, we only see a glimpse of these things. We practice resurrection by moving our bodies toward a Table, brushing elbows with other hungry and homesick bodies. Maybe those other bodies offended us in this past week. Maybe our relationships are strained. As a pastor, I have learned that this is more often the case than not. Every Sunday at church I see couples who are struggling to stay married or to stay connected with their kids. I see extended family members on opposite sides of a generational debate. I see colleagues who fell out at work but are working to restore their friendship. They all come, as I do, in need of supernatural help.

In the present world, our communion—with each other and with God—seemingly hangs by a thread. Sometimes it is completely invisible to us. But because Jesus has already been raised, it is a thread that holds. In him, Scripture tells us, all things hold together.[10] And by him, we are fed: not abstractly, but concretely. In our great vulnerability, we hold in our hands a small, tangible reminder of the One who is in fact holding us until he comes.

Some might see this description of hope as a kind of cop-out. Expecting present renewal alongside unmet longing is like trying to have your cake and eat it too. But if that's true, maybe there's more cake to go around than we've been taught. Maybe Christian hope offers a more expansive version of reality than the zero-sum. As others have articulated, Christianity teaches us to think less in terms of either/or and more in terms of both/and.[11]

My own experience bears this out. My persistent belief that God can and will heal creation has amplified my grief over the things he hasn't healed—my father, my family, my own lingering trauma-related dysfunction. But grief is not the enemy of joy. And in God's economy, sometimes our gains and losses function in reverse order. When we learn to hold our desires with open hands and offer them back to God with raw trust, he can make them—and us—into something more than we could previously imagine. He can bring renewal out of defeat, life out of death. This is, in fact, the mystery of our faith. We preach resurrection. Christ has died, Christ is risen, Christ will come again.

And in remembrance of him, Christ has commanded us to "take and eat."[12]

When we look to the host of our sacred meal, we see what hope looks like in real time. Jesus spent his ministry teaching that God delights to give good gifts to his children. He healed the sick, cast out demons, rebuked religious profiteers, and fed hungry crowds. He also, near the end of his own life, cried out to God with such desperate yearning that he sweated blood. Just before being handed over to death, Jesus prayed, "Father, if it be possible, let this cup pass from me; nevertheless, not as I will, but as you will."[13]

Jesus lived, and died, in the tension of trust. He asked for God's intervention while also surrendering to God's mercy in the face of suffering. Though Jesus was divine, he allowed himself to feel the existential angst of humanity when he asked in agony on the cross, "My God, my God, why have you forsaken me?"[14]

Our Lord has gone with us through the wilderness of *why*. He has endured the crucible of unmet longing. And he has made his own journey into an offering. Now, his death becomes our life. His loss is our gain. His wounds bring us healing.

Many historic Christian traditions call Communion by an older name: Eucharist. A shortening of the Greek word *eucharisteō*, which means "to give thanks," the Eucharist is fundamentally a thanksgiving meal. In taking the bread and wine, we receive again the good gift of Jesus' life poured out for us, and we thank God for incorporating us into that life—for making us, individually and together, members of Jesus' body.

Seen in this light, the Eucharist is not just a meal. It is the shape of the Christian life. Whether or not our prayers are answered in the short term, whether or not our stories turn out the way we hope, we can learn to give thanks to the One who shows what lies beyond our loss. We can learn to offer ourselves to God, fully confident that in Christ, even the cup of suffering can become the cup of joy. Jesus rejected the false paradigm of either/or; he now invites us to share in his ministry of both/and. He calls us to lives of hopeful surrender that can become, in God's hand, food for others.

When I think back to my dad's original interpretation of his cancer diagnosis, I see now that it was a bread crumb for me: a sign of something I didn't yet have words for but knew I needed. When I come to the Table, I understand. A life yielded to God is a eucharistic life.

2

ENCOUNTER

What Is Salvation Anyway?

It is Jesus that you in fact seek when you dream of happiness;
he is waiting for you when nothing else you find satisfies you;
he is the beauty to which you are so attracted;
it is he who provokes you with that thirst for fullness
that will not let you settle for compromise.

St. John Paul II, "Address of the Holy Father
John Paul II, Vigil of Prayer"

WE ARE ALL BORN LOOKING FOR SOMEONE.[1]

Before a baby can see much of anything, he gropes toward the familiar voice and smell of his mother. As his eyesight develops, he is first able to focus on an object about twelve to eighteen inches from his own face—roughly the distance between himself and the person holding him. By the age of three months, babies display a preference for faces with human eyes.[2]

When I was pregnant with my first child, I became captivated by the interpersonal nature of human development. With the help of a doula,

I prepared for a birth and postpartum experience that would optimize connection with our son. (In a word, I went the "crunchy" route.) Few things happened according to plan, however. A fast birth precipitated a postpartum hemorrhage and interrupted the initial skin-to-skin bonding time I'd wanted. My slow recovery was met with a host of nursing challenges, making for a difficult start to life together.

In the strain of those early months, what surprised and strengthened me most was my son's persistent desire for me. He didn't give up, so neither did I. Through blood loss, sleep deprivation, colic, reflux, and many, many tears, we became—slowly—mother and son.

Philosopher John Macmurray argued that the human instinct to connect is not only linked to our survival as a species; it reveals the nature of personhood.[3] Yes, babies will persist in desiring their caregivers because that is how they get their physical needs met. But also, through connection with his caregivers a baby becomes aware of himself as a person who is distinct from them and in relationship to them. We discover ourselves in and through the gaze of the other. This is not limited to childhood development. When my son was born, his gaze was as formative for me as mine was for him. Through relationship with him, I accessed more of myself. I became what he saw in me.

This becoming-through-relationship is part of what it means to be created in God's image. We do not exist as autonomous individuals but as persons in relationship with other persons. Recent neurobiological research seems to verify this. Our brains develop initially (and can later be regenerated) through interaction with other people.[4] We are made for—and even made by—connection with the other.

For many Christians, the notion that we are wired for relationship points to our need for God. Ultimately, his is the face we seek. Only through connection with him can we understand who we are. As St. Augustine famously prayed, "You have made us for yourself, and our heart is restless until it rests in you."[5] But when I reflect on my own Christian upbringing, I see the extent to which it was shaped by a different core message. Instead of God himself, I was taught to believe that what I needed most was God's "stuff."

In the late-modern West, almost all our interactions are shaped by transaction. We relate to the world as consumers, buying everything we need—whether it's the food we cook at home or the clothes we wear to work. Our social lives often revolve around consumption as well. We meet up to buy drinks or watch a movie; we discuss each other's wardrobes or latest hobby purchases or podcast finds. Thanks to the rise of technology and the ubiquitous use of social media, human connection itself has become a commodity that we consume. We solicit the gaze of the other through performance and transaction, sending "likes" to the people we hope will return the favor.

As persons wired for intimacy, we can't escape our relational instincts. But our transactional lifestyle has warped those instincts. In our desire to be seen and known by others, we unwittingly reduce *ourselves* to objects for consumption. We hope that if we can become attractive enough "products"—if we dress the right way or perform well at work or generally appear successful to others—we will secure our place in the world. We are what we buy; but also, we hope to be bought.

James K. A. Smith speaks to the formative power of what he calls this "secular liturgy" of consumerism. We are shaped, in our thinking and in our doing, by the transactional culture in which we live. Subconsciously, our hearts are formed by this "consumer gospel" and its promise that "goods and services will save you."[6] It shouldn't surprise us, then, when we realize that we've learned to relate even to God primarily as a distributor of goods and services.

Underlying many different Christian theologies is a common message: Trust and obey God to get something from him. The moral guidelines of purity culture imply that if you remain sexually pure, God will provide you with a spouse and a great sex life. Prosperity teachings often assure us that living a holy life will yield some version of health and wealth. Many popular Christian parenting programs suggest that if you raise your children according to the right principles, your kids will be well-behaved and grow up to make good choices. On a more subtle note, advocates for certain styles of worship or church governance might imply that if you are doing church "right," you won't be susceptible to the pitfalls and failures of other traditions.

We often embrace these formulas in good faith, from a desire to honor God and to make sense of the world. But insofar as these maxims shape our motivations, they cheapen our obedience by tying it to desired outcomes. They teach us to treat God like a divine vending machine, inserting whatever religious currency is required to buy the blessings we seek. Unwittingly, we often reduce the Christian life to a series of spiritual negotiations.

When I began pulling on the thread of my own transactional framework for faith, I was surprised to realize how deeply embedded it was. Permeating my understanding of the gospel itself was an exchange of goods: Give Jesus your heart and he will give you a ticket to heaven. As a child, I was deeply motivated by the get-out-of-jail-free theology that characterized my evangelical culture. As a young adult with authentic desire for others to know Jesus, I was drawn to the clarity and simplicity of a gospel message about repentance and rescue. Today I still see truth in it. Jesus died to forgive us from sin. I want my children to believe this. But I don't want them to turn to Jesus for what they can get out of it. In other words, I want them to want heaven because *he* is there, not the other way around.

There's a scene in the 1996 Christmas comedy *The Santa Clause* where two adults discuss when they stopped believing in Santa. The woman says, "I was [my young son's] age. I wrote Santa a letter every week that year. Okay. Maybe not every week, but . . . Boy, I really wanted a Mystery Date game. . . . Well, anyway, Christmas morning came and, oh . . . I got everything . . . except Mystery Date." The man responds, "I was three. And it was an Oscar Meyer Weenie Whistle. Christmas came, no Weenie Whistle. That's when I stopped believing."

This scene has stuck with me since my teen years. (So has Tim Allen's magically regenerating Santa beard.) Belief in God is more psychologically complex than belief in Santa. And yet I wonder if many faith crises include some version of this false premise: *If I'm nice, God will give me what I want.* When we don't get the things on our wish list, we assume that God must not be real after all. Or we discover that we're not all that interested in him apart from what he can give us.

When my dad was sick, our faith community sought to secure his healing through whatever forms of obedience God might require. In addition to pursuing medical treatment, we attended church faithfully and prayed fervently. Pastors anointed him. Our Christian friends all did their part to give my dad the best chance at survival. The first two years of his illness were marked by enthusiasm for the fight against cancer.

In the latter half of the battle, however, we grew weary. Hope for healing turned to plans for dying. Optimism gave way to grief and a slowly spoken goodbye. In the wake of his death, I felt confused and even angry at God for not giving us what we wanted. We had asked in faith. We had not cursed his name. We'd even planned to give God the glory for our happy ending. As a grieving fourteen-year-old, I blamed God for not holding up his end of the bargain.

But my disillusionment was undermined by another dynamic at work in my family's story. As I'd watched my dad's health decline over the last four years of his life, I watched his faith grow. His pursuit of God, initially catalyzed by crisis, eventually became an end in itself. Even though God wasn't answering his prayers in the way he wanted, my dad came to value prayer for other reasons. Somehow, even as his hope for healing waned, his hope in God deepened. After he'd been sick for a while, he wrote this prayer in his journal: *"Lord, I seek intimacy with you over healing—over anything in this life. Please teach me. . . . Lord, I seek you because you are worthy of my seeking. I do not seek you because of what you can do for me."*

This is not to say that he died placidly. His faith did not immunize him from grief or rid him of sin. Many parts of his story remained unhealed to the end. But overall, the trajectory of his illness was Godward. In the absence of God's "stuff," namely, the gift of healing, my dad had become captivated by God himself. For his tombstone, he chose Job 1:21: "Naked I came from my mother's womb, and naked I shall return. The Lord gave, and the Lord has taken away; blessed be the name of the Lord."

In my work as a pastor, I hear many stories of longing and loss. A young couple is trying desperately to conceive a child. A man is praying for redemption in his marriage. A celibate friend is wrestling with loneliness. A woman is grieving her adult son's addiction. A business professional is experiencing job loss. These stories can't be reduced to platitudes, and the hopes they represent shouldn't be dismissed as unspiritual or selfish. I don't think anyone who prayed for my dad's healing did so without authentic trust in the God who heard them. In the Bible, God invites us to ask sincerely for what we want.[7] Suppressing our desire—or even our disappointment with God—doesn't make us more holy; it only makes us less honest. But in all our longing, the challenge of faith is to not conflate the gifts with the Giver.

The Christian story, made tangible by a God who took on human flesh and lived among us, reminds us: The greatest gift God can give us is *himself*. His good news for the world is not an abstract message about salvation, the distribution of blessings, or even the offer of forgiveness. His good news is his promise to be with us forever.[8] Our forgiveness, though important, is in service of a greater end: it is the means through which we can experience union with God. Ultimately, our faith is not ordered toward the transaction of goods but toward the communion of persons.

We rehearse this truth in our worship when we gather around the Lord's Table. We come, hopeful or hurting, holding the unanswered questions of our stories in open hands. And in response, Jesus offers us himself. When I welcome the members of my congregation to receive the bread and the wine, I look in their eyes and think of all the assurances I want to give them—that their conflicts will be resolved, that their bodies will be healed, that their families will be restored in the ways they hope. I can't promise them these things. But I can give them something far greater: "the body of Christ, given for you."

The idea of union with God is not a new-age or modern invention. It is the most enduring theme of the Bible.

In the opening chapters of Genesis, God creates human beings to live in unbroken fellowship with each other, but also with himself. When sin fractures this fellowship early on, God's first question for his children is not "What have you done?" but "Where are you?"[9]

The redemption story that follows is God's own answer to that question. He takes it upon himself to find us and restore our closeness with him. Through Jesus, human beings are invited into a new, deeper communion with God than ever before—a communion so intimate that the Bible likens it to a marriage.[10]

This marriage, of course, is bigger than any one individual's relationship with God. Our rescue is not only personal; it is also corporate. God is redeeming a people for himself. This is one reason why the Lord's Supper is a communal meal: both now and forever, we are invited to enjoy God's presence *together*. As we practice this enjoyment, we remind each other that no earthly blessing, no human relationship, no created reality can fully satiate our longing. We were made for God.

In his classic memoir *A Severe Mercy*, Sheldon Vanauken reflects on his own "corporate" conversion to Christian faith alongside his wife, Davy. The couple met and married as young atheists, and later came to know Christ through the friendship and ministry of C. S. Lewis.

Early in their marriage, they had vowed to protect their "inloveness" above all other things and erected what they called the "Shining Barrier" to do so.[11] They promised to let nothing become more important to them than their relationship with each other.

But then they met Jesus.

At first, this seemed like merely a religious addition to their relationship. But over time, Davy began to love God so wholeheartedly, so single-mindedly, that Sheldon grew jealous. He felt, in a way, replaced. The irony in it was that in loving God more, Davy grew to love Sheldon better. She never faltered in her faithfulness or devotion to him, even though at times he did.

A few years later, Davy got sick. During her illness she prayed for her husband and that God would use her life in whatever way would draw Sheldon nearer to God. She sensed this would mean her death. She was right. Once doctors had done all they could for her, Davy died in a hospital bed while holding Sheldon's hand. She was forty years old.

After Davy's death, Sheldon wrote about his immense grief in letters to his friend and father in the faith, C. S. Lewis. In one response, included in the book, Lewis wrote to him: "You have been treated with a severe mercy. You have been brought to see . . . that you were jealous of God. So from US you have been led back to US AND GOD; it remains to go on to GOD AND US."[12] The rest of the book is Sheldon's journey to put this into practice: to learn, as Davy already had, to love God above all other loves.

What he realizes is that losing Davy—first to her newfound faith and later to death—ultimately saved them both. In subjugating their own marriage to a greater one, they found themselves "under the Mercy" of a God whose love was large enough to hold them forever.

In conclusion, he writes, "Only Love Himself with a severe mercy could breach the Shining Barrier and, by breaching it, save that guarded love for the eternity it longed for."[13]

A pastor of mine used to say, "The Christian life is one of ongoing conversion." At first, this irked the once-Baptist-always-Baptist in me that wants to emphasize our assurance in salvation; anyone who cries out to God will be heard by him, once for all. But eventually I understood that ongoing conversion is less about assurance of salvation than it is about a deeper, more holistic *experience* of salvation. In addition to our thoughts and beliefs, the Holy Spirit converts our loves so that we learn to desire God above all things. This is a lifelong process. We might initially be drawn to God because of what we believe he can give us—a ticket to heaven, a moral framework for life, a sense of community and belonging in the church. But over time, as we focus our gaze on him, we realize that he alone is the true object of our longing. "Man is a hungry being," wrote Alexander Schmemann. "But he is hungry for God. Behind all the hunger of our life is God. All desire is finally a desire for Him."[14]

In my own ongoing conversion, I've grown more aware of my desire for God above any abstract "blessings" he might give me. But simultaneously I've become more aware of my fear to express this desire for him. To seek God's gaze toward us, to crave connection and encounter with him, exposes our great vulnerability. It puts us in league with my newborn son, helpless but desperate for another's attention and attunement. In my desire to be seen and embraced by God, I feel safer trying to earn his affection through personal achievements or righteous living. I don't want to risk rejection. My ongoing conversion forces me to grapple not only with the question *Do I really want God (not just his stuff)?* but also *Does God really want me (without my accomplishments)?*

Perhaps my experience of childhood loss amplifies my fear of vulnerability. When our attachment with human caregivers is disrupted—or if it was never securely present to begin with—we might struggle to believe that there is indeed a loving Other looking for us.[15] Sometimes, even if we remain outwardly tough and detached, we turn that struggle inward and assume that we are not worth being sought. Esther Meek writes, "Scripture indicates that God intended palpable, touchable human faces and gazes in each person's life to prototype his own and most readily convey what Scripture indicates about the face of God. In this broken world, however, it may be that a person does not receive this from the conventional human sources—one's parents, one's spouse, or one's friends."[16] The quality of our interpersonal connections can either help or hurt our plausibility structure for connection with God.

I became aware of this dynamic in my life during seminary. As I was studying for the ministry, I slowly realized that I was more comfortable relating to God as my boss than as my Father. By my early twenties, I knew how to have an employer. I knew how to stay busy and earn my space in the room through productivity. But I did not have as much practice simply being enjoyed. I longed for connection with God but only knew how to seek it through usefulness to him. So I related to God primarily through tasks and even topics of study, because these were my methods of payment for his attention and presence. I subconsciously reduced our relationship to the transaction of information and service—hoping that if I could be useful enough, then maybe one day I'd feel worthy to just be in the room with him.

During seminary I also began receiving weekly Communion at my church. This practice introduced me to a different way of approaching God. Instead of coming to him with a task or a bit of information to dissect, I was invited to simply come. Empty-handed, without my books or my to-do list to hide behind, I was invited to be seen by God as I am. It was terrifying. And it was healing. At the Table I learned that in our vulnerability, God does not withhold himself or turn away. Instead, shockingly, he makes himself vulnerable in return. He says, "This is my body, given for you." His willingness to be wounded for our sake is what led him to live in a body in the first place. He became touchable, knowing that we would reject and kill him. And still, this crucified One offers himself. The giver has become the gift.

Many days, I do not recognize the value of this gift. I reject him in exchange for his blessings, or I cheapen his self-offering by assuming I can earn it through my good performance. But these things do not deter him. His gaze remains fixed in our direction, waiting for us to open our eyes. When we do, we realize that before we even knew to seek him, he was seeking us.

Christians often describe the redemptive acts of Jesus in terms of reconciliation: through his death and resurrection, we are reconciled to God.[17] To our modern ears, this implies a generic—or perhaps even a legal—sense of restored relationship. Through forgiveness, we are no longer at enmity with God.

But some scholars believe the English word "reconciliation" shares a history with the Latin word *cilia*, which means eyelashes. In being *re-conciled* to God, then, we can also imagine another, more intimate kind of relationship. Through Jesus, we are brought face to face, "eyelash to eyelash"[18] with the One we've been looking for all our lives. This intimate, personal encounter is the *telos*—the ultimate goal—of our faith. It is also the terminus of our quest for truth, beauty, and goodness writ large. Because at the center of these things is not a concept or an idea, but a person. To paraphrase philosopher Martin Buber, the heart of reality is not an "It" but a "Thou." So often we reduce our search for meaning, or even salvation, to the acquisition of an "It." Maybe this feels safer. An "It" cannot reject or challenge us. But we were made for more. We were made for communion.

On a personal level, I first began to understand this when someone in a white robe looked me in the eyes and gave me the Eucharist. In the vulnerability of that moment, I realized that the gaze I only knew in memory—that of a father delighting in his daughter—actually originated in another, living source. In the face of my priest, I came eyelash to eyelash not only with another human being but with Jesus Christ. I understood that there is a loving Other still looking for me, who invites me to not only know things *about* him or do things *for* him but to simply be *with* him. I am learning to believe this, and to return his gaze without fear or shame. This is, I think, the real work of the Christian life.

It's the work of our lives because on this side of Jesus' return, we continue to see his face as through a mirror.[19] We recognize him through prototypes, people who reflect to us the joy and safety of connection. We experience him through the ministry of the Holy Spirit who draws us and holds us in God's love. We encounter him in word and sacrament. And all these things teach us to yearn for the day when our faith will be made sight.

Every time I celebrate the Eucharist as a priest, I am instructed to make this yearning explicit. Our liturgy includes a prayer that those receiving Communion will experience the joy of union with Christ through the reception of the bread and wine, but also that they'll know him even more deeply when he comes again at the end of history. I pray: "Sanctify us . . . that we may worthily receive this holy sacrament and be made one body with him, so that he may dwell in us and we in him. *In the fullness of time . . . bring us with all your saints into the joy of your heavenly Kingdom, where we shall see our Lord face to face.*"[20]

At the start of this chapter I referenced Dr. Curt Thompson's suggestion that we are all born into the world looking for someone looking for us. He also says, "We remain in this mode of searching for the rest of our lives."[21] Our most primal psychological need reflects our most enduring spiritual hunger. In fellowship with Jesus, we taste salvation. When Jesus returns, our union with him will be complete and our hunger will finally be fully satisfied. Until then, our faith can feel like an ache and a fulfillment all at once. We have found the One we desire—or rather, he has found us. Even so, we pray, "Come quickly, Lord Jesus."

3

EMBODIMENT

Broken Bread for Broken Bodies

Every lament is a love song.

Nicholas Wolterstorff, *Lament for a Son*

When I got married, I didn't know how to boil noodles.

At least, that's the story. Maybe it wasn't quite that bad—but I did come into marriage without much cooking experience. I'd only lived on my own for two years, in a house with other busy young adults who rarely had time to sit down for meals together. It seemed like a lot of work to learn how to cook—and clean—for one. So I mostly stuck to sandwiches and the occasional fried egg. My more culinary housemates sometimes shared their fare with me, which provided superior nutrition to my standard lunchmeat but also proved that better food could be had if I was willing to do the work. I was not. Until I found myself setting a table for another. Suddenly, boiling noodles seemed both relevant and necessary to the welfare of someone I loved. Getting married changed my relationship with food—and, by extension, my relationship with embodiment in general.

Like many American Christians, I grew up without a very robust theology of the physical world. God made it, so I knew it was "good," strictly speaking, but material creation didn't really enter the conversation beyond that.[1] Aside from specific moral commands regarding how to live in our bodies and how to treat the bodies of others, it seemed that God's real concern was with our souls—the spiritual, immaterial part of us that is housed inside our physical frame. This is the part of me I believed would be "saved," whisked off to a disembodied heaven after death. When my father died, my great consolation was not that his body would be resurrected and renewed but that his spirit would live on, immaterially, forever. If anything, it was a *sin* to love the body too much—to fixate on the husk of the real, redeemable center of a person.

Odd as it may sound, cooking for my husband (and his cooking for me, which admittedly was the tastier option at first) called this paradigm into question. As I learned to lovingly feed the body, I began to understand what generations of moms and grandmothers have demonstrated with their after-school cookies and Saturday pancakes and perpetual second helpings: to feed the body *is* to feed the soul. Somehow, the spiritual and material parts of us are not as distinct as I once thought.

Orthodox theologian Alexander Schmemann also recognized food as an entry point to a more integrated way of understanding the world. He wrote,

> Centuries of secularism have failed to transform eating into something strictly utilitarian. Food is still treated with reverence. A meal is still a rite—the last "natural sacrament" of family and friendship, of life that is more than "eating" and "drinking." To eat is still something more than to maintain bodily functions. People may not understand what that "something more" is, but they nonetheless desire to celebrate it. They are still hungry and thirsty for sacramental life.[2]

I was not a secularist; I believed in something more. But I didn't realize the "something more" of Christianity had anything to do with the food on my plate. I grew hungry for sacramental life when I started to connect the dots between my embodied existence and God's redemptive purposes. This had little to do with formal, churchly sacraments at first. But I knew I needed a bigger frame for my faith—a spirituality that incorporated the material world rather than dismissed it.

The tendency to denigrate physical creation isn't new. It's actually quite old. In the ancient world, it was common to pit material realities against spiritual ones. Some prominent philosophies even taught that the physical world was evil, a prison from which to escape.[3] In those views, the soul was good but the body was bad.

It's easy to see how these ideas contributed to religious understandings of salvation as escape from the physical world into the immaterial, spiritual one (namely, souls in heaven). But this was not the message of the early church.

From its birth, Christianity was good news not just for souls but for "wholes," as N. T. Wright puts it.[4] Instead of demeaning material creation, ancient Christians bore witness to its rescue through the ministry of Jesus. His resurrection showcased God's ultimate future for human bodies. And he instructed his followers to worship him through bodily practices like baptism and the Eucharist.

In fact, the church fathers saw the sacraments as proof that salvation extends to our bodies. In response to those who denied this, Tertullian wrote, "How can [they] allege that flesh is incapable of the gift of God, . . . seeing that the flesh is fed on the flesh and blood of the Lord and is a member of him?"[5] In Jesus, God comes to us materially, to redeem us materially. He gives his body to our bodies.

This conviction also put matters of social welfare on par with sexual ethics in the early church. Theologian Christopher Hall argues that for the earliest Christians, "to denigrate the body would undercut our concern about what we do with our bodies *or* the suffering of others in their bodies."[6]

If Jesus has come to renew all things, then the way we treat all things has moral implications.

For me, cooking for someone I loved was the gateway to understanding how a physical reality could simultaneously be a spiritual one. Once I conceded that, I wanted to uncover all the ways God might convey his love to and through our bodies. I wanted to understand how, and why, the things of heaven could be intertwined with my experience of earth.

Christian faith is sometimes described using the language of paradox—a truth that seems, at first, like a contradiction. We believe in one God who is also three persons; who exhibits both justice and mercy; who taught that losing one's life is the way to find it and that suffering can be the path to joy. The Christian God delights in expanding our categories. And in his chief act of self-disclosure, the incarnation, we encounter another paradox: the immaterial God has become a human being. Jesus Christ makes the invisible God visible.[7] For Christians, then, redemption begins and ends not with an escape to heaven but with heaven wedding itself to the stuff of earth.

Jesus took up a body to renew creation, not to rescue us from it. We continue to experience the difficulty of embodied life on earth, but the New Testament describes this as an effect of sin, not a feature of the physical world per se. Our hope, the apostle Paul tells us, is that one day, "the creation itself will be set free from its bondage to corruption."[8]

Even though the incarnation may seem like old news to modern Christians, it continues to challenge us. God's choice to become permanently one with creation by indwelling a human body settles any remaining questions we may have about the importance of the material world. God made it, which makes it good, but also God has definitively acted to rescue it from corruption and decay. The flesh-and-bone, resurrected, fish-eating body of Jesus is proof that tangible creation is neither evil nor irrelevant. Instead, it is redeemed.

Earth was designed to be "crammed with Heaven," as Elizabeth Barrett Browning wrote.[9] When we believe this, we learn to live in our bodies with less suspicion and more expectation. Instead of experiencing earthly life as one big potential temptation or distraction from more important "spiritual matters," we learn to welcome God's presence in and through the world he made. The feel of water on our hands, the taste of cheese, the embrace of a friend—these can all enrich our worship of the God who made himself touchable for our sake.

For many of us, thinking about the incarnation can still feel a bit abstract. But the primary way Jesus invites us to remember him relies less on abstract thought and more on muscle memory. We chew and swallow him. We taste his sweetness on our lips. We receive his body with our bodies. The sacraments convey his love to our senses. Through the tangible means of bread, water, and wine, God speaks to us in a language that both precedes and outlives our cognitive reasoning. In this way, God is as much like a mother who lovingly feeds her children as he is like a teacher who instructs his students.

I'm still working out the implications of this. When my young sons—who were baptized as infants[10]—began asking to take

Communion, I feared that they were only interested in it because they thought it would taste "yummy." My pastor at the time said, "Yumminess is actually a great starting place." To this day, my seven-year-old spends extra time marinating his bread in the grape juice at our church. He is learning to taste and see that the Lord is good. So am I.

We will never fully understand the mystery of the God-man or his love for us. But we can take and eat.

When I was training for ordination, my first congregation was a small group of residents at a nursing home down the road from our church. Once a month, we transformed their multipurpose room into a sanctuary for a time of worship and Communion. A roll-top bedside table donned a white tablecloth for bread and wine. One of the residents played some favorite hymns on the piano. I practiced greeting and preaching to members of God's family who didn't speak as fast as I did or who didn't speak much at all anymore. Then I assisted the minister in distributing the Lord's Supper. We walked slowly through each row of worshipers, stooping so that they could receive the bread in their wheelchairs. Some of them just opened their mouths for us to feed them. After the service, we visited those who were bedbound. Even those who were too frail to sit up or otherwise communicate with us still welcomed the small wafer dipped in wine. In this simple way, they communed with God. They received his love tangibly, tasting on their tongues a promise of resurrection.

Sharing Communion with these elder saints challenged me. It revealed that our bodies are not only valuable to God insofar as they are "useful" to him or only if we keep them out of trouble. He does not privilege some bodies over others. Young or old, chaste or disgraced, we are holy ground. We are the place God longs to dwell. His love and rescue will leave no part of us behind.

The problem, of course, is when our own bodies tell us otherwise.

Like many women and men, I grew up receiving a variety of messages about my body. Some of my earliest memories include my dad brushing my hair before bed and warming my bare feet with a blast of hot air from the hair dryer. These simple sensory pleasures showed me what love felt like on my skin. It was safe and warm and a little bit ticklish.

But a few years later, I received different sensory messages from the hands of others. The first time I was sexually violated, I was still young enough to not really understand what was happening. As is often the case, a trusted adult assured me what he was doing was normal and that I should relax. I tried to comply, but my body resisted. My muscles tightened and my eyes watched the door silently, pleadingly, for someone to walk in and make it stop. Or maybe I imagined that I was already on the other side of the door and not trapped in this moment. Either way, that experience planted the seed of dissociation in my story.

When I couldn't resolve the cognitive dissonance between what my mind was told and my body knew to be true, I sought to escape the tension by leaving my body behind altogether. Then and for years afterward, I subconsciously prayed a version of Psalm 55:6, "Oh, that I had wings like a dove! I would fly far away and lodge in the wilderness."

My experience is not unique. Over half of all women are sexually abused in their lifetimes, and almost one in three men.[11] But even those of us who have not been physically violated have still been on the receiving end of derogatory comments, degrading images, or have otherwise been made to feel "less than" in our bodies. We were humiliated when our parents were rough with us or when peers made fun of our acne or the size of our nose. We remember realizing that, despite our best efforts, we don't look like the people on the magazine covers. Some of us were told our skin is the wrong color. In a thousand small ways, we carry not only love in our bodies but also shame. And pain. And disease.

Regardless of what we believe about embodiment and resurrection, our lived experience often speaks a louder word. Our joints ache. Our cancer recurs. Our kidneys fail. Our vulnerability is visible in our stooped shoulders and sagging skin. And even what can't be seen by others often screams at us from the inside. Trauma experts teach us that our bodies store painful memories[12]—that grief and stress and shame aren't just emotional constructs; they live in our cells.

In a world where all things remain subject to corruption, living in a body can be exhausting. It's often embarrassing. And it inevitably ends in sadness. My dad died at age forty-four, but even if he'd been cured of cancer, he would still have ended up in a coffin eventually. Death is unavoidable. No matter how privileged, healthy, loved, or educated someone is, he or she is still going to die.

To live in a body is to suffer, one way or another. In light of this, it is understandable that we gravitate toward theologies that downplay our pain. We minimize—or perpetuate—bodily harm by reasoning, "it's *just* my body." We even put a positive spin on death by reframing it as a kind of graduation day, an escape to a better place. Which, in a way, is true—for now. In Christ, to be absent from the body is to be present with the Lord.[13] On the cross, Jesus told the thief who repented, "Today you will be with me in paradise."[14] Though our bodies decay, God does save our souls. This message offset my despair as I watched my father's casket disappear into the ground. But insofar as I lacked imagination for a future bodily redemption, I settled for a half-truth that stopped short of biblical comfort. Because the larger picture the Bible paints is one in which death itself will be undone. Death is not something to be polished with promises of a spiritual afterlife; it is an enemy to be defeated.

This hope is sometimes harder to hold because it is delayed in coming.

In the here and now, it's easier to denigrate the body than it is to persevere in yearning for its wholeness. This is no truer for those of us who grieve the death of a loved one than for those of us who live with sin's other personal effects in our bodies. In the presence of chronic illness, unwanted sexual desire, or other dysphoric experiences, we feel the groan of creation viscerally, and we grow weary. Over time we might be tempted to suppress our hope for relief or even to tune out physical sensations altogether in favor of a cleaner, more manageable spiritual life. Dissociation, it turns out, is less painful than lament. It's less messy too. But the inherent goodness of our bodies, and God's promise to redeem them completely, compel us to cry out, "How long, O Lord?"[15]

When I began exploring the impact of sexually exploitative experiences in my life, I realized that some of my theological privileging of the "spiritual" realm over the physical was actually a smokescreen for my shame. I subconsciously assumed that my body was the problem—or, at least, that it was not a problem God wanted to solve. To attend to my body's brokenness would be to open a can of grief and confusion that seemed antithetical to the things he instructs us in his Word to think about; whatever my bodily reality was, I would not have described it as good and pure and praiseworthy.[16] So I baptized my contempt in a subtle, spiritual forgetfulness of my physical self.

Through food, both domestic and divine, Jesus put me back together. In my marriage, he prepared a table for me that opened my heart to come to the other Table with a hunger I'd carefully suppressed for most of my life. As I received the bread and the wine at church, I began to understand that Jesus did not shed his blood merely to purify my ideas or to rescue my soul. He gave all of himself for all of me. It's not "just my body" if Jesus died for it. My body is me, and I am precious to him. I am the place he longs to dwell. This means that the *real* me, the person Jesus came to save, is not somehow separate from the face I see in the mirror.

I both loved and hated this realization.

It was healing to discover that what happens to me on earth matters profoundly to God, and that he will restore what the "locust" of abuse and cancer and death has eaten from his children.[17] But this promise of renewal also required a fuller reckoning of what the locust had eaten than I wanted to give. It required me to stare my shame in the face so that it might be healed.

A few years ago, I had the opportunity to lead a healing service at my church. It was one of the most meaningful experiences I've ever had. In my tradition there is, of course, a liturgy for this (Anglicans love a good script), and I was both intrigued to discover it and excited to share it with my congregation. Our church family included many who were wary of conversations about miracles and healing. Whether due to hurtful previous experiences, an upbringing that underemphasized (or overemphasized) the miraculous, or merely a personal worship "comfort zone," I knew that some who attended our first healing service came as much out of curiosity as anything else.

I was genuinely surprised, then, by how many of them came forward to be anointed and prayed for at the conclusion at the service.

Those requesting prayer walked single-file down the aisle just like they would on a Sunday morning to receive Communion. But unlike most Sundays, many of the people who came forward were crying. As they knelt at the low wooden rail at the front of the church, they shared stories with me dating back to their childhoods, or of chronic pain that no doctor could explain, or of afflictions so private they chose to share them with me in writing rather than speak them aloud.

Silent tears streamed down their cheeks. Couples clung to each other. One woman grabbed my hand as I prayed, desperate. Their corporate show of emotion revealed to me: When we welcome our bodies into the conversation about redemption, they have a lot to say. We're so practiced at suppressing the grief and shame our bodies carry that we're often not even aware of the story they're telling.

But God became flesh to heal our flesh, not to distract us from it.

Some people who came to the healing service that night experienced miraculous recovery. Others saw no change in their symptoms. But all of them left more fully known. When I saw them again the following Sunday at church, I remembered their stories and how they'd courageously shared them a few nights before. And as they came forward again, this time for Communion, I placed bread in their hands as evidence: Jesus welcomes their broken bodies with his own.

When Christians celebrate the Lord's Supper, we are not recalling an abstract message of love or forgiveness. We are remembering Jesus' *actual* life poured out. This meal, then, perhaps more than anything else, gives us courage to face the shame that clings to our flesh—because it tells the story of a God who lived in the flesh with us.

When we stare into the void of bodily harm and humiliation and suffering, we see not an empty hole waiting to swallow us, but the scarred hands of Jesus waiting to embrace us. Jesus, who also lived in a body that was subject to corruption and decay. Jesus, who also was also violated and abused, mocked while hanging naked on a cross. Jesus, who did not spare himself the sadness or pain of death; who wept at the tomb of his friend, and who later could not dry his mother's tears as she watched him die. When we break the bread, we remember that Jesus' death was not only the purchase of our redemption. It was also a profound act of solidarity with us in our suffering. Our priest and mediator is also our companion in the pain. He knows what it feels like to be broken.

Claude Atcho reflects on how African American poets have expressed this as they've grieved lynched Black bodies in the American South. In their lament, they have seen Jesus "from below," from the perspective of those who have been brutalized or who have been forced to watch, with horror, the violence done to their loved ones as they hung from a tree. He writes,

> When we gaze from below—that is, when we see who and what the suffering see when they gaze upon the crucified Jesus—our view of Jesus becomes more whole. We find that Jesus is not simply transcendent but immanent, concerned not simply with heaven but with earth. Jesus is not a heavenly bystander to our suffering; he stands by us in the fiery furnace then and now.[18]

This is the true scandal of the incarnation—that God assumed not only our material nature but also the extent of its sorrow and shame. He went to the depths of human suffering that he might meet us there and then raise us with him. There is no painful memory, no physical or psychological agony, no dark tomb that remains outside his reach.[19]

This realization has changed the way I participate in the story my body is telling. Instead of praying, as I once did, "Oh, that I had wings like a dove so that I might fly away," I am learning to *also* pray, "Where can I go from your Spirit? . . . If I go up to the heavens, you are there; if I make my bed in the depths, you are there. If I rise on the wings of the dawn, if I settle on the far side of the sea, even there your hand will guide me, your right hand will hold me fast."[20]

This realization has also changed the way I engage the stories of other bodies. Instead of turning away from the physical suffering of others, Jesus' own example compels us to stand with them in solidarity. His passion is the foundation for our compassion, our commitment to "suffer with" those who experience bodily harm.

We don't need to fear the darkness of lament—our own, or anyone else's—because Jesus sits beside us in it. He understands, not abstractly but concretely, all the complexity and pain of embodiment. He is God with us. Edward Shillito, a pastor in Great Britain during World War I, said it this way in his poem *Jesus of the Scars*:

> If we have never sought, we seek Thee now;
> Thine eyes burn through the dark, our only stars;
> We must have sight of thorn-pricks on Thy brow,
> We must have Thee, O Jesus of the Scars.
> The heavens frighten us; they are too calm;
> In all the universe we have no place.
> Our wounds are hurting us; where is the balm?
> Lord Jesus, by Thy Scars, we claim Thy grace.
> If, when the doors are shut, Thou drawest near,
> Only reveal those hands, that side of Thine;
> We know to-day what wounds are, have no fear,
> Show us Thy Scars, we know the countersign.
> The other gods were strong; but Thou wast weak;
> They rode, but Thou didst stumble to a throne;
> But to our wounds only God's wounds can speak,
> And not a god has wounds, but Thou alone.[21]

The God who suffers in solidarity with us is unique among all world religions. And his wounded body speaks a better word than any sermon. But when we remember his body, given for us, we also remember his resurrection. The bread we break tells the story: "Christ has died, Christ is risen, Christ will come again." Jesus' victory over the grave is evidence that our hope for physical renewal is not just wishful thinking. He is what the Bible calls the "firstfruits" of our own future, the proof that our wounds will not win.[22] In him, even death will be undone. One day we will live in our bodies without pain or shame, and creation itself will be freed from the specter of decay.

I, and everyone I know, still wait for this.

Though we experience renewal now, we continue to live with the fallout of sin and the sting of death. We groan as we anticipate our adoption as risen ones.[23] But while we wait, we take and eat what Olivier Clement called "resurrection food."[24] In the meal God has prepared for us, we feast on a future that is breaking into the present, bringing healing and renewal to the most hidden parts of us. Because Christ's body was broken for us, our bodies can be made whole.

It's a promise we apprehend by faith; but even now, it's a promise we can taste.

4

GIFT

The Prophetic Practice of Joy

———————

*And he sang to them, now in the Elven tongue, now in the
speech of the West, until their hearts, wounded with sweet
words, overflowed, and their joy was like swords, and they
passed in thought out to regions where pain and delight
flow together and tears are the very wine of blessedness.*

J. R. R. TOLKIEN, *THE RETURN OF THE KING*

IN THE FIRST FEW YEARS AFTER LOSING MY DAD, I embraced
sadness as an act of loyalty.

Allowing myself to feel happy, or even lighthearted, seemed like
a kind of betrayal. As if enjoying the sunrise or laughing during a
movie would diminish his loss or imply that I was moving on. I
subconsciously vowed to honor him through a commitment to
being miserable, even though I knew he wouldn't have asked this
of me. Grief is weird like that.

As I matured, I realized that grief, though nonlinear, has many
stages and usually lifts over time. What feels like loyalty morphs:

Initially we may see joy as a threat to our sense of loss, but later we welcome joy in honor of the one we loved. A friend of mine lost her young daughter in a tragic car accident on her first day of sobriety from drugs. In the agony of the following months, what kept her from relapsing was a fierce commitment to honor her daughter's life by staying sober. She has done so. Years later, she celebrates her stability as an act of devotion to the child she lost.

At its best, grief can have an expansive effect on our lives. Through loss, we learn to live more courageously because we know there are no guarantees. We've counted the cost of love, and we choose to pay it anyway. But at its worst, grief can crystalize around our hearts and prevent us from feeling the thrill of love at all. Suffering can make us strong, but it can also deaden us to joy. This is a double-edged sword: developing grit is a grace, but not if it comes at the expense of hope.

In my life, this has been subtle. Most days I am grateful for the anvil of adversity—God has used it to shape me into something sturdy. But sometimes I become aware of my covert expectation that adversity is all there is. Having experienced hard seasons, I sometimes struggle to believe that there is also good in store for me. Tragedy is more plausible than happiness. I no longer cling to sadness consciously, but I often expect it by default.

When I was pregnant with my second son, I was plagued with fears of stillbirth. Despite a healthy pregnancy and a thriving toddler already at home, I couldn't shake the idea that this new child was going to die. With some help from a counselor, I realized that I could rationalize *one* happy ending—one healthy child seemed permissible. But who was I to think God would give me another one?

As I've examined this assumption, both in my own life and in caring for others who struggle to receive good gifts, I've discovered it has multiple roots: a low view of self or a low view of God, or both. In the movie *Blood Diamond*, we see how self-hatred can stem from but also perpetuate trauma. Early in the film, schoolboy Dia Vendy is kidnapped from his home in Sierra Leone and trafficked as a boy soldier. He is given drugs and guns and used as a weapon of war. His father, Solomon, searches for him. When they meet, Dia points his gun at Solomon as if to shoot. Through tears, his father addresses him:

Dia, what are you doing? Dia! Look at me. . . . You are Dia Vendy, of the proud Mende tribe. You are a good boy who loves soccer and school. Your mother loves you so much. . . . I know they made you do bad things, but you are not a bad boy. I am your father who loves you. And you will come home with me and be my son again.[1]

The father reinterpreted his son's story by clarifying: Bad things happened to you, but that is not because *you* are bad. To our modern ears, this message might seem obvious. And yet, in our God-given need to make meaning of our lives, many of us subconsciously internalize painful experiences as somehow our fault, or what we deserve—and, therefore, what we can expect to continue happening. We need to hear the voice of the Father say, *these bad experiences do not define you or your future.* Even the bad experiences we bring on ourselves are powerless against the grace that makes us daughters and sons.

Another cause of worst-case scenario thinking stems from mistrust of the Father himself. How can we believe his promise of good when he did not uphold it in the past? How do we know he is truly loving or truly capable? As a teenager in a single-parent household trying to figure out how to pay for college, I felt much more comfortable trusting myself to get a job and pay off loans than I did trusting God to provide what he already clearly *hadn't*. I didn't doubt his character as much by that point, but I did doubt his competence. In my young adult years, I often saw God as a kind of nice guy who had good intentions but wasn't reliable with follow-through. To view God this way, I later realized, is to live like a functional atheist. It's possible to profess faith consciously but to subconsciously operate as if God doesn't exist. In this framework, the future is entirely up to us.

The deep irony in this for me was that while I was busy doubting God and trying to solve life for myself, God was busy providing countless opportunities, connections, scholarships—and yes, also loans and jobs—that in retrospect I had to acknowledge as gifts of grace. Even the nonreligious recognize there is more at work in the world than our efforts. As Michael Lewis told Princeton University graduates at their 2012 baccalaureate, "Life's outcomes, while not entirely random, have a huge amount of luck baked into them."[2] My faith deepened when I learned to see God not only as the source of *un*answered prayers in my life, but also as the source of my life's many gifts. In his sovereignty, God allows us to experience hardship. But in his generosity, he also gives measureless blessings. What we might want to attribute to good luck or hard work remains covered in God's fingerprints.

Every good thing comes, ultimately, from above.[3]

When I examine my life through this lens, I realize that his goodness shines brighter, and is more pervasive, than any tragedy. Its ubiquity is the very reason we don't tend to see it: Every breath, every birdcall, every blade of grass is a gift. God's kindness is the connective tissue of reality. It holds all things together, buoying each *no* of our lives in the overarching *yes* of love. This does not diminish the realities of suffering and loss, but it embeds them in a larger portrait of grace. And it teaches us to live prophetically, clinging to joy even when it is temporarily obscured by grief.

My mom might be the best example of this in my life. When I was in seminary, I asked her which psalm I should choose to preach on for a class assignment. Given the challenges of losing her husband to cancer and raising six kids on her own, I expected her to pick something heavy. The Psalms are full of lament, grief, and questions for God. But her suggestion surprised me: "Why not Psalm 16? It's my favorite." I looked it up and read,

> The LORD is my chosen portion and my cup;
>   you hold my lot.
> The lines have fallen for me in pleasant places;
>   indeed, I have a beautiful inheritance. . . .
> You make known to me the path of life;
>   in your presence there is fullness of joy;
>   at your right hand are pleasures forevermore. (Ps 16:5-6, 11)

My mom's enduring identification with joy—despite her acquaintance with grief—piqued my curiosity. Because I know her well, I know her outlook isn't based in denial or distraction. Phony cheer is cheap but also short-lived. True delight is deeper, a bedrock that holds even when our circumstances don't. It's a prophetic posture that challenges our assumptions about how life works—and that reveals something about the life to come.

In October of 2020, while the world was reeling from the coronavirus pandemic, I preached at a wedding. We bundled up for an outdoor ceremony, awkwardly refrained from hugging despite our excitement to see each other, and then cried happy tears for our friends getting married. After months of relative isolation and in the middle of a very serious time worldwide, it was jarring to celebrate such a joyous occasion. We'd been practicing lament for almost a year, and appropriately so. The bride, who worked as a nurse in a major urban center, knew this more intimately than most. But this couple's staunch commitment to new life was also appropriate.

As I watched them make vows, I was reminded that some things can't be killed by disease or even death. Love will outlast everything we can't control. Their wedding was a prophetic moment, bearing witness to the fact that in the sweep of history, sorrow will not have the final say.

We especially need this kind of witness during difficult seasons. And yet, in our effort to be sensitive to the painful realities in our midst—or in our zeal to point beyond them—we often miss the mark. We either fall short of believing that light overcomes darkness, or we deny the darkness altogether and lose credibility with those who suffer in its shadow. To err in one direction makes us Eeyores, moping about everything that's wrong with the world. To err in the other direction makes us Pollyannas, irritating others with our naive positivity.

If I'm honest, my tendency to lean too heavily toward positivity or despair fluctuates by the day—and not for profound reasons; usually, it has something to do with how much sleep I got the night before. We are fragile creatures. This is one reason why we worship corporately: Together, we are more capable of telling the whole truth. But our worship also helps us as individuals to internalize the truth. By rehearsing the story of redemption week after week, we buttress our hearts against the ebb and flow of our personal narratives.

When I come to church and I'm having a bad day, I remember that there is more to the story than my immediate experience. Whether we find ourselves grieving or rejoicing, together we remember that joy wins, but not without a fight. The sorrow we experience is as real as the scars on our Savior. But now he sits, renewed, at his Father's right hand—and while we remain in the presence of our enemies, he prepares a table for us.

In the early church, the Lord's Supper was a fairly serious affair. Persecution hung in the air as both a threat and a memory. Christians gathered for worship sometimes with fresh grief after the imprisonment or martyrdom of a friend. Perhaps in part for this reason, the earliest eucharistic liturgies all begin with an invitation called the *Sursum Corda*, which the officiant would extend to the congregation: "Lift up your hearts," or more literally, "Hearts up!" The congregation would then respond, "We lift them up to the Lord." Ancient Christians believed this sacred meal transported them, mysteriously, to a heavenly realm that remained out of death's reach—a realm that one day would be fully present on earth.[4]

This belief even led them to celebrate the Lord's Supper on the graves of martyrs, partaking of the feast that they'd one day share again with their departed loved ones.[5] It wasn't a denial of their grief, but a commitment to look beyond it. It was a subversive joy that both enraged their persecutors and contributed to the church's rapid growth in the first three centuries.

Coming to the Table doesn't diminish the heaviness in our lives. But it does lift us beyond it, to taste for a moment the joy and lightness for which we are headed. This joy then strengthens us to face whatever grim realities we must endure in the meantime.

In his first miracle, Jesus modeled something very similar. By providing wine at a wedding feast, he began his own ministry with the end in mind. Before turning his face toward Jerusalem to stare down the challenge of the cross, Jesus sponsored a party. In his sermon "Lord of the Wine," Tim Keller said, "By turning water to wine Jesus reveals the whole purpose of his ministry. It's as if Jesus is telling us, 'Yes, I've come to do self-denial and to suffer and to be humbled, and you will too if you follow me; but those things are means to an end. The end is the *feast*.'"[6]

In the long struggle of faith, it is easy to forget that God is not a taskmaster—he is a banquet-master. Keeping the feast at the center of our worship helps us to remember. When we come to the Lord's Table, we practice "lifting our hearts" again and again, until the ritual of joy gives way to its reality. It's our dress rehearsal for eternity, and eternity begins now.

A few years ago, I had the privilege of giving my friend's five-year-old daughter her first Communion. We met the week beforehand to talk through the meaning of our special meal at church. She wiggled in the wrought iron patio chair outside Starbucks as she told me how the bread reminds us of Jesus' body and how she wants to follow him. The following Sunday, I invited her and her family to the front of the church to receive Communion ahead of the rest of the congregation. She pranced forward, resplendent in a light pink ball gown and glittering ballet flats. I wondered if she might be nervous in front of so many adults; but she beamed at me as I put the small wafer in her hand. She showed us all what it looks like to begin with the end in mind.

As I study the shameless joy of children, I sometimes envy them. I assume that stoicism is an inevitable aspect of maturity; that what I must have known intuitively as a kid is lost forever, and rightly so. We grow up and realize that the world is not a playground. People aren't always nice, and the good guys don't always win. Relationships can be irreparably broken. Poverty and racism persist. With adult eyes we think we see the unvarnished truth.

But there's a reason Jesus told his disciples that if they want to enter the Kingdom, they need to become like children. Because God's new world operates differently than ours does. It requires us to unlearn what we think we know, so that we can apprehend what is now true in light of Jesus: The dead are raised. The lame walk. The blind see. Wars cease, captives go free. My kids have no trouble believing this stuff. Every night at bedtime, my six-year-old prays that he'll be able to fly tomorrow. Though I always add to his prayer a special request for protection from false starts, there is something of resurrection in his quest. He understands that with God, nothing is impossible. And though his prayer remains unanswered, he seems undeterred in his hope that one day, he might fly.

In his fictitious *Letters to Malcolm*, C. S. Lewis suggests that activities we might consider childish or frivolous are actually the best analogy we have for understanding the character of heaven: "While we are in this 'valley of tears' . . . certain qualities that must belong to the celestial condition have no chance to get through, can project no image of themselves, except in activities which, for us here and now, are frivolous."

He admits his own difficulty with this, as one who "never enjoyed any game and can dance no better than a centipede with wooden legs." Nonetheless, he argues that we tend to assess things according to the wrong values in our "upside down" world. He says "that which, if it could be prolonged here, would be a truancy, is likest that which in a better country is the End of ends. Joy is the serious business of heaven."[7]

I respect Lewis's honesty. And I would have liked to see him dance. If he's right about joyful play as the "End of ends," I imagine I will see him dance one day. In the meantime, his words challenge me to welcome celebration with as much reverence as I might practice lament.

I've watched a handful of women grieve a death in their family while caring for young children. On the one hand, they had to fight for space to feel sad, to rage, to get quiet with their thoughts. On the other hand, they also had to continue playing hide-and-seek, cooking dinner, and taking the dog for a walk. To sit with death while stewarding life is to live in two worlds. It can feel like being torn apart, or like being asked to lie half the time. But if we give ourselves to the tension—if we apprentice joy even as we grieve—we might become *more* whole as a result, not less. When we embrace what might feel frivolous or false in the moment, we stay tethered to a truth that will outlast the moment. For grieving moms, this is an opportunity born of necessity. For the rest of us, it's a discipline.

The church calendar helps with this. Since at least the fourth century, Christians have organized their worship around the story of salvation by retelling it in church throughout the course of the year. Staying alive to the whole narrative requires that we commit to seasons of both fasting and feasting. However, the year's longest season of fasting is punctuated by an even longer feast. Lent's forty days of penitence gives way to fifty days of Easter to remind us— whether we feel like it or not, we are people of the party. Our faith is ultimately ordered toward celebration. The feast trumps the fast.

And in case we forget this truth in the long dark of Lent, every Sunday leading up to Easter is a feast day, a whisper of the resurrection that waits just around the corner. (A friend of mine went through at least two rounds of Lent before being notified of this. She felt robbed, in retrospect, of all the chocolate she could have eaten on those Sundays.)

Authentic Christianity forbids us from diminishing sin's gravity or its effects. We are compelled to grieve and cry out for rescue. But even more so, we have reason to rejoice because that rescue has come. Right now, our rejoicing might feel a little bit like play therapy. We go through the motions, acting out what we've heard about the good news even when it seems disingenuous. We are training for the serious business of heaven.

In my tradition, when a priest officiates a Communion service, we call him or her the "celebrant." Christians *celebrate* the Eucharist. Historically, this meant Christians gathered to solemnly receive the Eucharist—"to celebrate" didn't adopt a joyful connotation until the sixteenth century—but I like the double meaning it holds today. Our fellowship around the Lord's Table is both serious and celebratory. We honor Jesus through our worship, and we joyfully receive the gift of his life in and among us. We recount his death in all its gravity, and we boldly profess our hope in his resurrection. The Anglican church in Kenya refers to the Eucharist as "the feast of victory." The bread reminds us that Jesus is victorious over death—and in him, we will be too.

Usually when I preside at Communion, I believe every word I'm saying. But occasionally my historic doubt creeps in. What if all of this is just wishful thinking? What if Jesus is actually still in the ground somewhere? The idea that we'll all be raised to feast with him forever sounds too good to be true. Sometimes I feel like a poser in church because what *seems* more real to me is the old creation, not the new. Death and disappointment are what I know. The feast of victory is what I hope for. Sometimes resurrection reads more like a fairy tale than a biography.

On those days, after leading the liturgy and introducing the Supper, I then feed my own failing imagination with a taste of bread and a sip of wine. Even as the celebrant, I am first and foremost a recipient of this gift. It is as solid and distinct from me as the cup in my hands. This story is not of my own making, and it does not fluctuate with my feelings or my faith. Jesus is raised whether I can bring myself to trust it today or not. And yet, he is patient with me. As the poet George Herbert said, "though my soul draws back, Love bids me welcome."[8]

When we are out of optimism, afraid to hope, or even struggling to believe, we are still invited to come, empty-handed, to the feast. Salvation is a gift, and all we bring to it is our reception. Sometimes we even get that a bit wrong, but in his kindness, God gives us grace to receive him again and again. At the Lord's Supper, we rehearse the truth that there is good in store for us, that however our stories started or even how we perceive them to end, there is another end of

ends—a celebration where the wine will never run out. The more we
internalize this, the more we begin to joyfully participate in it now.

Joyful participation takes time to learn because, as Tish Harrison
Warren wrote, "in this fallen world, joy is risky."[9] Skepticism can
feel safer, even if we've been at this a while. I often slip back into my
old ways of thinking, licking my wounds and wondering whether
God can be trusted. But the weekly practice of coming forward for
the Lord's Supper, putting my body in the way of hope even when
my heart lags behind, is changing me. Because every time, my outstretched hands are filled. Every time, it's a little bit easier to believe
that he has made good on his promises, that his resurrection is
more real than what I can see with my eyes and that in him, all the
sad things will come untrue.[10]

There's a beautiful painting that hangs in the Musee d'Orsay in
Paris depicting Peter and John running to Jesus' tomb on Easter
morning.[11] Mary Magdalene has just told the disciples that Jesus is
alive and they must see for themselves. One might expect pure excitement on their faces as they race to find the risen Lord. But instead,
the artist conveys a mixture of longing and fear in their raised eye-
brows and clasped hands. John, the younger of the two, had been
Jesus' most faithful disciple—with him to his last breath on the cross,
ready to receive Jesus' mother as his own. Now he wonders: *Could
this news possibly be true? Or will I be made a fool in my hope?* Beside
him is Peter, the one who denied his Lord. His confidence had turned
to cowardice after Jesus was arrested. He clutches his heart and scans
the horizon, hoping: for a second chance? for forgiveness? Missiol-
ogist Mike Frost calls the painting "a study in desperate anticipation."[12]
My sister calls it the picture of her faith.

It has always been risky to believe the good news. We struggle
to trust that mercy triumphs over judgment and that life will over-
throw death. But we are invited to embrace that risk, to run toward
it—even if we continue to wring our hands along the way.

5

COMMUNITY, PART 1

The Table That Makes a Family

---

*The church is perhaps one of the few places left where
we can meet people who are different than we are
but with whom we can form a larger family.*

HENRI NOUWEN, *REACHING OUT*

WHEN MY SIBLINGS AND I USED TO FIGHT, my dad would
sometimes interject by saying, "One day your brothers and sisters
will be your best friends. They are the only people in the world
with the exact same blood as you." I thought this was a strange
argument, but its somewhat graphic (bloody) nature made it stick
in my mind regardless.

We continued to fight, of course, but over time I did begin to
appreciate the unique bond my siblings and I share. Nobody else
walked through those years of cancer and death, of slow loss and
slower readjustment, from the same vantage point as we did. Together we carry a corporate memory. The particulars are unique to
each of us, but there's enough commonality in our lived experience

that no explanation is needed for the tears that still sometimes come, or the silence, or the reassuring text messages: "Home safe. Love you." In my brothers and sisters, I literally see myself—and my father—in the characteristic square jaw and broad smile we each inherited from him.

For all our foibles, we are a family. We are not alone in our stories.

Growing up after our dad's death, we sometimes *felt* alone, together. Grief and loss are isolating experiences, and the awkwardness of adolescence didn't make things easier. Our situation was incomprehensible to most of our peers. In high school I resented that some of my friends' biggest concern in life was their social status, but I also envied them for it. I wanted to feel as intact as they looked. I wanted normalcy as I perceived it.

Of course, in a broken world, loneliness *is* normal. This has less to do with our circumstances than our interpretation of them: We assume, regardless of the reason, that we are alone in our struggles. *Nobody understands. Nobody else is failing this badly. Nobody can be trusted.* These lies are as old as sin and the fig leaves we donned in response. The evil one used my family's crisis to plant the perception of isolation and otherness in my mind; in reality, my family's crisis revealed how connected and cared for we were.

Matthew's Gospel tells us that early in Jesus' ministry, someone interrupts his teaching to inform him that his mother and brothers are waiting outside to speak with him. He responds by saying, "'Who is my mother, and who are my brothers?' And stretching out his hand toward his disciples, he said, 'Here are my mother and my brothers! For whoever does the will of my Father in heaven is my brother and sister and mother.'"[1] Jesus isn't snubbing his family with this comment—he's expanding its definition by counting as kin all who obey God the Father as he does. He co-opts deeply ingrained beliefs about family loyalty and belonging, then reappropriates them in relation to himself. Jesus' teaching here and elsewhere in the Gospels lays the foundation for Christians to refer to each other in familial terms. Through our shared relationship to the Father, we are brothers and sisters.

When I was a struggling, lonely teenager, I experienced the meaning of Jesus' words before I understood them. A small army of adults claimed my siblings and me as their own, not through biology but through faith. We were mothered and fathered and sistered by those who did the will of God in caring for us.

This began when my dad was sick, with people who took us into their homes for extended periods of time while my parents traveled for treatments. And the care we received continued well after he died, when financial crisis compounded our grief and left us vulnerable to further hardship. Our Christian school awarded full scholarships to all six of us so that we could finish school where we started. A Lutheran church in town rented their parsonage to us after the bank foreclosed on our family home. Anonymous friends dropped bags of clothes on our front porch. A Sunday school teacher from church met me weekly at school to tutor me so I wouldn't fail ninth grade, the year my father died, and continued to mentor me after that until college. Church friends took my youngest brother to father-son camps with them and their own sons.

In myriad—tangible, costly—ways, the church created a social safety net for my family, offsetting the fallout of tragedy in our lives by catching us mid-fall. It is not an overstatement to say that I am probably a Christian today because of the ministry of these men and women, some of whom are still anonymous to me. The church quite literally helped raise me.

In my work as a pastor, I've come to see that the grace I received as a child is not unique to me. When the church is functioning in the way God intended, it is tacitly "familying" those in its orbit. Empty nesters give up their quiet Sunday mornings to volunteer in the nursery or teach Sunday school. Busy moms cook double-batch dinners so they can bring a meal to a bereaved or struggling family. Young adults mentor high schoolers. Men work together to repair an elderly couple's roof or mow their lawn.

Most of these things happen under such ordinary auspices we barely notice it. It is the quiet miracle of life together. As miracles go, it would be easy to explain these things away, to attribute them to generic altruism or moral obligation—but its power lies in the fact that it does not originate with us. The miracle of the church is that because of Jesus, strangers are born again as siblings. Through participation in him, we now have the exact same blood as each other. For "the cup of blessing that we bless, is it not a participation in the blood of Christ?"[2]

It is no secret that Christians cherish the nuclear family.

Fidelity to Jesus has always included faithfulness in one's human relationships, beginning with one's family. The New Testament is full of instructions for spouses, parents, and those with elderly relatives.[3] Church leaders are vetted in accordance with how they treat their households.[4] Christians believe the family was created by God and given to the world as a gift: through these primary relationships, human beings are literally born from, and into, love. We are nurtured in community and experience the safety of commitment. As sisters Lilo and Nani explain in Hawaiian terms in Disney's *Lilo and Stitch*, "Ohana means family, and family means nobody gets left behind." This is a universal good that reflects a universal ache.

However, in our zeal to defend the importance of familial bonds, Christians have sometimes elevated the family to an almost

idolatrous level. We have unwittingly implied that ultimate fulfillment is found in these human relationships, as fragile as they are.
And in the last century especially, we've privileged a certain expression of family as the measure of Christian success. An unspoken maxim of American evangelicalism is that varsity-level
Christians are married with children. In college, an older single
friend of mine was devastated when a church leader told him he
would never be able to go into ministry without a wife and kids.
Since college, I've counseled countless women whose prolonged
singleness or infertility triggered an identity crisis.

When evaluated in the light of Scripture, many of our modern
Christian "family values" seem somewhat ironic. Though marriage
was held in honor and children were received as a blessing, New
Testament Christians valued singleness as an equal—if not a superior—Christian calling.[5] And though biological ties were treated
with reverence, they were embedded within, and in some sense
peripheral to, a much larger family: the household of God. This
larger community was preeminent for Christians, re-ordering their
individual households so that husbands and wives, parents and
children, masters and servants had to learn new ways of seeing and
relating to each other as brothers and sisters. The overwhelming
majority of familial language in the New Testament speaks of this
new, spiritual family, the church.[6]

God's people have always known themselves in some sense as a
family. The Hebrew Scriptures describe Israel as both God's son
and his bride.[7] Israel's prophets compare God's love for them with
that of a father, and elsewhere of a mother.[8] But this familial connection to God was understood *primarily* as a corporate reality:
Israel, the nation, was God's son.[9] Additionally, Israel's familial

relationship with God was preserved through its ethnic line. To belong to God's family, one must either be born Jewish or assimilate to cultural Judaism.

Jesus introduced two radical developments to this. First, he taught *individuals* to call God Father, as he himself did. Through Christ, Israel's King and the unique Son of God, we now share a more intimate, personal sonship—we learn to cry "Abba."[10] Second, Jesus instructed his followers to extend this privilege to people of all nations, regardless of their ethnic identity. The result was a new community of people whose allegiance to Jesus might have displaced them from their biological families and who now had to learn to live together as a people constituted not by a common history or lineage but by a common faith.

Membership in this new community was marked by a rite of rebirth (baptism) and its worship was organized around a shared table (Eucharist). From its inception, the church understood itself as a family into which children are "born again" by the Spirit and water, and who are nourished through fellowship with Christ and each other. This is why many church sanctuaries and cathedrals still feature a baptismal font at the entrance and a Communion table at the center. A Christian worship space is a family home.

In the first few centuries of the church, following Jesus might have meant the loss of ethnic kinship or family favor. This remains the case in many countries around the world today. But Jesus promised that this loss would not be total: "There is no one who has left house or brothers or sisters or mother or father or children or lands, for my sake and for the gospel, who will not receive a hundredfold now in this time, houses and brothers and sisters and mothers and children and lands . . . and in the age to come eternal life."[11]

I did not lose any of these things for the gospel's sake; my family cracked under the strain of life in a broken world. But by grace, I was still grafted into a network of fathers and brothers and homes that ultimately enriched my life by a hundredfold.

Family relationships can never be replaced. People are not expendable. The primacy of the church in a Christian's life does not imply that biological ties are unimportant or that they can be abandoned due to preference. Those who have neglected their children or spouses in the name of "the church" are accountable for their failure to love the first congregation God has given them.

But the God and Father of all does teach us to look beyond the natural bonds of kinship and realize that broken or not, our little families cannot adequately contain his love. We need the larger family of faith to help us understand the mystery of our inheritance, our identity as those born "not of blood nor of the will of the flesh . . . but of God."[12]

In other words, the church is not just the failsafe for families who fall short of the ideal. The church *is* the ideal. In this light, I sometimes understand childhood loss as having given me an advantage. Human parents, however loving or healthy, are insufficient. Their ministry is partial, a pane of a window into the love of the Father. I would have needed other fathers and mothers and sisters and brothers even if my dad had never gotten sick. Cancer was simply the catalyst in bringing this to my awareness. We all need more faces than those in our family—faces that don't look like us but that turn toward us anyway—to gain a fuller picture of God. And if we are to grow up into his image, we need opportunities to practice turning toward others in return.

In the early church, these opportunities to practice were ample. Especially at the Lord's Supper.

Before the legalization of Christianity in the fourth century, virtually all Christian worship took place in homes, and the earliest celebrations of the Eucharist happened in the context of a full meal at a domestic table.[13] These weekly suppers were sometimes called "agape feasts" because they were an expression of the highest form of love: God's love for us in Christ, which paves the way for a new kind of love for each other.

This community of love was revolutionary in the ancient world because it blended diverse ethnic and socioeconomic groups and taught them to relate to each other in entirely countercultural ways. Jews and Gentiles learned how to break bread together. Wealthy landowners and poor slaves learned how to share a meal equitably. Christine Pohl writes that the agape meals of early Christian communities "were distinguished from the contemporary practice of offering elaborate banquets that reinforced status boundaries. . . . These meals were intended to reflect transformed relationships in which worldly status distinctions were transcended, if not disregarded, and formerly alienated persons could view themselves as brothers and sisters at God's table."[14]

This new dynamic created plenty of drama, both within the church and without. But it also contributed to the church's rapid growth in the first three centuries. Disadvantaged members of society especially were drawn to a fellowship where their status was determined by faith, not by their social rank—where its teachers insisted "there is neither Jew nor Greek, there is neither slave nor free, there is no male and female, for you are all one in Christ Jesus. And if you are Christ's, then you are Abraham's offspring, heirs according to promise."[15] Church historians point to the church's profound growth as a primary reason that eucharistic celebrations evolved from a household meal to a public ceremony: It eventually became untenable to fit everyone in a small space.[16]

Most churches today continue to observe the Lord's Supper as a ceremonial meal apart from a full supper. But this does not diminish its sociological import. Whether we come forward to kneel at an altar rail or pass trays of little plastic cups from seat to seat, the fact remains: Our shared fellowship with the Father makes us a family. We may have different backgrounds, bloodlines, or politics, but we are one in Christ Jesus. As a kid, I remember watching every adult in my Baptist church tip their heads back to drink their grape juice at the exact same moment. It was a nonverbal indicator that communion with Christ is a corporate reality—and it made me want to share in it. As personal as salvation is, our communal supper reminds us that belonging to Jesus also means belonging to each other.

Christians have spent centuries discussing the meaning of the Lord's Supper using what Peter Leithart called a "zoom lens"—we want to zoom in on the table and know what's happening (or not happening) to the bread and wine. As an Anglican priest, I get jazzed about this conversation. But if we focus on this to the detriment of the "wide-angle" lens, if we pay attention to the communion elements or our personal experience of them but fail to see the people gathered around the Table and what the meal means for us as a community, we are missing out on a central aspect of the Supper and of Jesus' intention for it.[17] The communal nature of the meal reminds us that whatever is happening at the Table, it isn't only happening for me: it is happening for us.

A friend of mine, a Baptist pastor, once discussed this issue with a Roman Catholic bishop. Despite their different "zoom lens" perspectives on the nature of the Lord's Supper, they agreed on the importance of helping their congregations understand how the Supper informs our corporate life. Even in the Roman Catholic tradition where the Eucharist is highly treasured, the bishop told my friend that there are still many in his church who "risk

approaching the Lord's Table as a party of one with little thought
of the grander view of the great big family table."[18]

It seems that, for Christians of every theological tradition and
denomination, the call is the same: If we want to honor the body
and blood of Christ, we begin with looking our brothers and sisters
in the eyes and learning to love them as he does.

For college, I moved about a thousand miles away from home.

During orientation weekend my freshman year, my mom picked
out a local church for us to visit (as moms do). I went along, though
what I remember most about the service was how tired and dis-
tracted I felt while sitting in the velvet-cushioned pew. Making
such a big move had disoriented me. My mom noticed this and
wanted to see me off with at least one church connection. What
neither of us knew at the time was this church had a specific out-
reach to college students and that it would become my church for
the four years I lived there.

It started with lunch.

Each Sunday during the school year, this church hosted an ecu-
menical "Campus and Community Service" designed to integrate
various campus ministries with local Christians of all ages. At the
conclusion of worship, we gathered downstairs for an informal celebration of Communion followed by a free, hot meal. It was a bril-
liant strategy that kept me coming back and even gave my spiritually
ambivalent friends a reason to try church. But it also helped me to
experience the Eucharist in a way I never had before. Growing up,
the Lord's Supper was a reminder of Jesus' love for me as an individual. But in this new context, it also became an expression of
Jesus' love for—and through—a community.

Their liturgy was very simple. We stood in a circle around the room while the pastor offered a brief explanation and a prayer. Then we took bread and grape juice from the hands of church volunteers who'd prepared it for us. Being in the round allowed me to see the faces of Christians who'd been following Jesus for longer than I'd been alive, and who were organizing this service specifically to support me in my faith. It gave me an imagination for the body of Christ being not only in heaven at the Father's right hand or mysteriously in the bread I held but also in the room with me around the circle. Jesus' body is his church.

This body loved us well. They embraced a huge, hungry group of college students and provided a kind of family we would never be able to find on campus—an intergenerational fellowship where retirees and elementary schoolers and young professionals all had reasons to share their lives with each other.

One family in particular shared their life with me during the week as well, first by hiring me to babysit but later by making me an honorary relative. I spent many evenings in their home after my babysitting shift had ended, where I received many more free hot meals. At first, witnessing the intact fellowship of a family up close exposed the great ache I still felt at having lost access to this in my own life. I found myself staring awkwardly at times at the mundane interactions between father, mother, and children, longing to experience those interactions personally. I no longer could, of course, as a biological daughter.

But over time, this family's inclusion of me changed the way I experienced that longing. And the fellowship I shared at their table helped me begin to understand what it means that God also welcomes me to his table—not as an employee but as a guest. And even more than a guest, a daughter. The lines between the domestic and the ecclesial blurred during those years as I was nourished at the "great big family table" of faith. This season brought the needed healing for me to one day become a mother to my own children. And it caused me to fall deeply in love with the local church as a place where mothers are not only made by nature; they are also given by grace.

In an article for *The Atlantic*, David Brooks chronicles the short season in American life when families abandoned larger relational networks in favor of a new ideal: the detached two-parent home. He describes that fifteen-year experiment between 1950–1965 as "a freakish historical moment when all of society conspired, wittingly and not, to obscure the essential fragility of the nuclear family."

Smaller and more fragmented versions of family life were marketed as an expression of financial success and personal freedom. People moved away from their extended families; they built houses with bigger bedrooms and smaller front porches. But as societal trends toward individualism and autonomy continued, the isolated two-parent family imploded under the stress. Today, Brooks argues, only the wealthiest Americans can survive under this model because they alone can afford to hire all the help that extended families used to provide.

Rather than attempting to resuscitate a historically abnormal way of life, Brooks suggests that the path forward lies in rediscovering our need for "extended clans," kinships that are strong enough to support the smaller, nuclear family unit. He concludes:

> Americans are hungering to live in extended and forged families, in ways that are new and ancient at the same time. This is a significant opportunity, a chance to thicken and broaden family relationships, a chance to allow more adults and children to live and grow under the loving gaze of a dozen

pairs of eyes, and be caught, when they fall, by a dozen pairs of arms. For decades we have been eating at smaller and smaller tables, with fewer and fewer kin. It's time to find ways to bring back the big tables.[19]

When I first read Brooks's article, I couldn't help but think of the big table at the center of Christian faith. Through Christ, we are grafted into a family large enough to absorb our personal crises or losses. We don't necessarily live in the same households, although many Christians are exploring creative ways to do this. But regardless of where we live, the communion of the church contains our little families, like nesting dolls, within itself—not eradicating our natural bonds, but embedding them within the broader community.

For those of us with broken or painful experiences of natural family, this is a form of rescue and rehabilitation. Through baptism into the Father's name, we are born again into a new family dynamic. We are seated at the table of fellowship with God's own Son, who teaches us how to live as renewed sons and daughters. Old stories of dysfunction or disillusionment lose their power as we are "re-familied" together. Experiences of isolation and loneliness are healed as we practice belonging to him and to each other. In the church, orphans become heirs and childless men and women become spiritual mothers and fathers.

It would be dishonest of me to suggest that this happens easily or seamlessly.

But I remain captivated by the fact that this is our birthright.

In the world Brooks's article describes, it is also our mission. As biblical scholar Brenda B. Colijn wrote, "If we can figure out how to be a truly redemptive family, we will have something very important to share with a fragmented society. May it be so."[20]

6

COMMUNITY, PART 2

When God's Family Contributes to Our Pain

———————

"Things usually work out in the end."
"What if they don't?"
"That just means you haven't come to the end yet."

JEANNETTE WALLS, *THE GLASS CASTLE*

BEFORE MY DAD GOT SICK, I thought he was invincible.

At least, he was the largest human being I'd ever known. A former football player, his 6'4" frame was, in my view, almost as broad as it was tall. On childhood vacations, I remember trailing behind a large group of family members in the crowded Atlanta airport—but unlike Kevin in *Home Alone 2*, I didn't get lost because my dad's head and shoulders remained easily visible above the hordes of other travelers. He was larger than life to me. His death enshrined this perception, and perhaps even enhanced it.

Dying almost always improves one's reputation among the living.

But as I grew into adulthood, I learned that my dad was less invincible and more complex than I once perceived him to be. Like all human parents, he had his flaws. Some were quite profound, but my age at the time prevented me from seeing or understanding them. Similarly, I used to see my entire family through the rose-colored lenses of childhood: I thought the relationships in our extended network of siblings, cousins, aunts, uncles, and grandparents were happy and uncomplicated. What I have since realized is that even the happiest families have their share of dysfunction. There is no human community untouched by human brokenness and sin.

In an essay for *The Point Magazine*, Tish Harrison Warren wrote, "If you were wildly in love with church as a kid, it's a confusing and painful thing to grow up."[1] On the other side of childhood, many Christians live with a kind of cognitive dissonance about our faith family. We met Jesus through the church—but also through the church, pain and disillusionment. We discovered that our leaders aren't the heroes we once thought they were. We learned the Christian history of imperialism, colonialism, racism, and other -isms that defy Jesus' explicit teaching. We watch our brothers and sisters insult each other in defense of their political ideals. We personally suffer, sometimes profoundly, at the hands of other Christians.

Even outside of Christian circles, one of the greatest barriers to faith in Jesus can be "the problem" of the church—Jesus might be appealing, but his people often aren't. Many Christians, out of fidelity to Jesus, wonder how they can stay with the family that continues to betray and misuse him.

And yet, Jesus himself has refused to be separated from his people.

In Saul's famous conversion story from the book of Acts, he is on his way to hunt and kill Christians in Damascus when he is knocked to the ground by a heavenly light and a voice saying, "Saul, why are you persecuting me? . . . I am Jesus, whom you are persecuting."[2] From the church's birth, Jesus has so closely identified with his people that when they suffer, he suffers. He is resolute in associating with us, even when it hurts his reputation.

This is not to say that Jesus glosses over the church's sins. Some of his harshest words in the New Testament are reserved for the people who misrepresent him.[3] God seems to have created a tension between his promise to indwell his people and his promise to destroy and judge evil.

This is a tension we are called to live with as well.

In his classic work *Life Together*, Dietrich Bonhoeffer argues that Christian community is both a necessity and a grace. Writing in the context of Nazi Germany, where the threat of dispersion and imprisonment for those who opposed Hitler was imminent, Bonhoeffer cherished the chance to live among the seminarians he taught at Finkenwalde for two years. (After this short time, their project was shut down by the Gestapo.) Bonhoeffer treasured their togetherness and knew its vulnerability to outside forces. And he argued that any proximity with other Christians, even if for a brief visit in prison or for a time of prayer, is a foretaste of our future when God will gather his people from "the four winds."[4] We need each other, and the privilege of being together should result in praise "from the bottom of our hearts." He writes, "Let them thank God on their knees and realize: it is grace, nothing but grace, that we are still permitted to live in the community of Christians today."[5]

But in the same work, Bonhoeffer also articulates the dangers of idealizing Christian community. Our togetherness is a gift, but that doesn't make it perfect or even easy. Rather, our proximity to other Christians is a gift in large part because it keeps us aware of our need for mercy. Through our recognition of each other's failures, we become disillusioned—and this is a good thing:

> Just as surely as God desires to lead us to a knowledge of genuine Christian fellowship, so surely must we be overwhelmed by a great general disillusionment with others, with Christians in general, and, if we are fortunate, with ourselves. . . . Only that fellowship which faces such disillusionment . . . begins to be what it should be in God's sight, begins to grasp in faith the promise that is given to it.[6]

If we stick around long enough in any community, we'll experience disillusionment. What makes disillusionment with the church more painful is that when other Christians hurt us, God is somehow implicated as well. These are the people we've looked to as an expression of divine love. We expect more from the church than from the rotary club, and we should; this is the family of God.

But, Bonhoeffer suggests, we should also expect that the church will still let us down. (His own experience of other German Christians who supported Nazism illustrate this painful reality.) And when the church fails, we don't need to deny our disillusionment to protect anyone's reputation. Nor do we need to suppress our disillusionment for fear of losing faith in God's family. Rather, we can integrate these difficult feelings into a deeper understanding of the church's true identity: we are a people who, from the beginning, have fallen terribly short of our aspirations as followers of Jesus.

We are *not* God. We are a people who need his rescue.

Most of the time, we work really hard to obscure this fact. Individually and corporately, we like to think of ourselves as exemplary— or at least above average. Most Sundays, whether I am sweating through church as a mom with little kids in tow or sweating through church as the pastor up front, I try to look normal. *Everything's fine. We're all getting along fine.* The truth is often much less picturesque.

In reality, my kids barely made it to church this morning with pants on. The pastors up front are barely on speaking terms. These things make us uncomfortable because they challenge the ideal that we badly want to project—so we all play along to protect each other from the fact that we are not okay, and we don't know how to fix it. As Mike Cosper wrote regarding self-deception in the church, it's "easier to cherry pick reality than watch a dream die."[7]

Church, of course, is not the only place we do this. In an image-conscious world, we are trained in keeping up appearances from childhood. Already, my seven-year-old is worried about how his hair looks before school. Whatever labels we use to describe ourselves, whatever tribe we claim as our own, we fear being exposed as a failure or a fraud—so we feign competence and satisfaction. We cherry-pick a narrative we can feel good about. *Everything's fine. We're all getting along fine.*

Ironically, church has become the one place I can find respite from the façade. However much I've been pretending through the week or even on my way through the door, at church I am invited to kneel with my brothers and sisters and confess the truth. We have fallen short of our ideals for ourselves, we have sinned "in thought, word and deed."[8] In God's presence we receive mercy—not as the people we wish we were but as the people we actually are. This gives us courage to face reality, to watch our dreams for ourselves die, so that we can take up God's dream for us instead.

Christians have been confessing sin in church for as long as we have a written record of worship, because our life together is predicated on the fact that we are going to get it wrong—a lot. As much as I need to confess my own sins, I need to remember that the person next to me is also a sinner who will let me down and probably hurt me. I need to remember this about my pastor, and he needs to remember it too. Our fellowship begins at the foot of the cross where we all stand guilty and in need of renewal.

And then, our fellowship continues around a family Table where we practice living together as forgiven and restored siblings.

⟶🐦

In my church tradition, we never share Communion without first "passing the peace." This is a moment in the service when we celebrate God's forgiveness by extending it to each other. By grace, we enjoy peace with God. This reality then compels us to seek peace with each other. Usually on Sundays, passing the peace feels more like a halftime stretch break than anything else: The extroverts among us shake as many hands as possible and the introverts sneak off to the bathroom. Once, during a vow-renewal ceremony I officiated for a married couple, the peace began with an enthusiastic kiss—after which the rest of us cheered.

But this ancient practice is more than a liturgical palate cleanser; it is essential preparation for the Lord's Supper. In the early church, Christians who were at odds with each other were expected to reconcile before receiving the Eucharist.[9] They understood this as obedience to Jesus' teaching that our relationship with God is connected to our relationship with others: "So if you are offering your gift at the altar and there remember that your brother has something against you, leave your gift there before the altar and go. First be reconciled to your brother, and then come and offer your gift."[10]

Sharing table fellowship with Christ means being ready to share that same fellowship with his people, including those who have offended us. It also means that if we want to commune with Jesus, we don't get to do that apart from our brothers and sisters. As Fleming Rutledge said, "There is no other way to be a disciple of Jesus than to be in communion with other disciples of Jesus."[11] He invites us to a *family* table. Even though it might feel a lot less complicated, there is no option for a "just Jesus and me" Christianity.

At the same time, coming to the family table does not imply that we excuse or deny sin for the sake of our fellowship. Passing the peace allows us to name our disillusionment with each other as part of our worship. And it prevents us from papering over conflict or wrongdoing because it reminds us that reconciliation costs something. It requires that we recognize how we have failed each other; and it requires that we forgive.

Of course, some sinful behaviors are so grievous that forgiveness can only happen from a safe distance. In cases of abuse or chronic mistreatment, when it becomes clear that the larger community is either unable or unwilling to address the wrongdoing, the godliest thing to do might be to leave one church and worship somewhere else. This, too, can be an outworking of God's peace. After we've done all that depends on us in pursuit of restoration, we are free to find a different community where healthier relationships can take place.

Whatever shape it takes, passing the peace is hard work. It takes courage to name offenses and seek reconciliation. It takes humility to apologize and ask forgiveness. It takes discernment and grit to leave a church we've loved and open our hearts to a new one.

It's much easier to sweep our grievances under the rug—or to walk away from church altogether. But Jesus' own example shows us a different way. In righteous anger against religious corruption, he flipped tables in the temple. He was unafraid to tell the truth about sin even when it made a scene. Despite what we often see in Christian circles today, Jesus never concealed or even downplayed his peoples' wrongdoing. If anything, he called attention to it—for the sake of their healing and growth. And then, before ascending to heaven, he promised to never leave or forsake them.

Throughout the church's history, Jesus hasn't left. He has stayed present among us—without condoning our sin. This is the legacy we are each learning to follow, in small and big ways. We will never do it perfectly; we are apprentices of grace and truth. Our fellowship will be fraught as long as sin remains. But in this way our life together is an expression of the gospel. We fall short, we discover grace, and we are reconciled—to God and to each other. Again and again and again.

Confessing our sin and passing the peace are requisite practices for Christians—whether we enact them liturgically on Sundays or not—because none of us will ever graduate from needing grace. Hopefully, we get better at recognizing this about ourselves over time, and we become quicker to repent. However, this is not always the case. Sometimes the process of reconciliation is impossible because one or both parties refuse to acknowledge their wrongdoing. In every family, occasionally there are stalemates. Sometimes those stalemates include the family leaders—a matriarch refuses to forgive a prodigal child; a father refuses to acknowledge his sins against his children. In the church it's no different.

A few years into my ministry as a pastor, I was invited to share my story at a local college campus. An interdenominational student group was interested to hear from ministers in various traditions and professions, and at six months pregnant, I represented a (very) small niche of pregnant-mom-priests. I expected to get questions about women in ministry, discerning a call to ordination, and what it means to be Anglican. But near the end of the meeting, a young woman asked me a question that I was not prepared to answer: "What about ministry has most surprised you so far?"

I was not prepared for her question because my answer wasn't particularly pleasant. What I wanted to say—and what remains true years later—is that what has most surprised me is how much sin and corruption I've encountered among Christian leaders. Going into ministry, I knew Christians in general (myself included) can be toxic and dysfunctional. But I did not realize that the shepherds (myself included) are often just as dysfunctional as the sheep. I thought, or at least hoped, that those entrusted with leadership in the church would be a bit further along than the rest of us. Thankfully, many of them are. But the reality is that, from top to bottom, the church is a family full of fledgling, wayward children.

And it raises the question: What if the people leading us in confession and peace are also the ones committing sins against their people and are unwilling to recognize it? What if the whole process of reconciliation breaks down because those with religious authority refuse to be held accountable? As a leader in the church, I am haunted by this question. And I am challenged by the fact that God has baked accountability into the meal I serve his people.

In the very earliest description we have of the Lord's Supper being celebrated in church, the apostle Paul warns those who partake of the bread and wine to examine themselves and "discern the body"— to ensure that they are treating each member of the community with the same respect they would give Jesus' own body—lest they eat and drink judgment on themselves.[12] In the Corinthian church that Paul was addressing, there was a pattern of inequity between the wealthy and poor members of the congregation: those who had plenty to bring to the eucharistic celebration ate in excess, while the poor members of the church who had nothing to contribute to the feast went hungry. Paul condemns this as antithetical to the example of Jesus, who gave up what he had—his very body—for others.

As Jesus' followers, we must come to the Table with the same spirit of self-giving and love for our brothers and sisters. We must be ready to acknowledge where we've fallen short of this and to repent. To fail to do so is to eat the Supper in an "unworthy" manner and to be guilty concerning the body Jesus gave up for us. This means, as Methodist theologian Laurence Stookey wrote, that "at the Table of the Lord the church is both judged and strengthened by Christ, the Host. The assurance of forgiveness, so often associated with the Eucharist, is legitimate only when we know that forgiveness is for the penitent, and penitence is literally a 'turnaround' that involves change."[13]

Without repentance, the bread we break is not to our comfort. It is to our chastisement.[14]

I don't understand exactly what it means to eat and drink judgment on myself. But I know that as a church leader, I am not exempt from it. Pastors and leaders who refuse to see their sins against Christ's body will still be held accountable for them— whether we witness it in our lifetimes or not. Jesus himself has promised to do this. For those who have been harmed by Christians without apology, this is a strange consolation. Regardless of the cost, Jesus will do right by his body. Each time we come to the Table, we are called to do the same.

As I've grown in my appreciation for the Lord's Supper over the years, I've become aware of another aspect of the church's failure to experience it as God intended: In our denominational divisions, we have failed to remain in communion with each other at one shared Table.

Growing up Baptist in the South, I didn't think much about different denominations. Virtually everyone I knew—including Jesus himself, surely—was Baptist in one form or another. But after high school, two of my siblings converted to Roman Catholicism. Suddenly, the Protestant Reformation was being relitigated in my family. During the first few years that we worshiped in different traditions, I became painfully aware of the fact that we could no longer take Communion together.

Since then, I've come to know and love other Roman Catholic Christians, whose tradition restricts them from celebrating Communion with Protestants. And I've witnessed church divisions within

Protestantism that have created deep relational rifts between Christians with differing convictions. Even when separation happens for important reasons, it remains something to lament. Whenever and however Jesus' family is divided, we fail to experience the unity and fellowship that he died to give us. His body, already broken for our sins, is further torn apart by infighting and schism.

There aren't easy answers to this. But in my own life, I might not have even become aware of the problem if I had not been in relationship with Christians from different theological traditions. Though I cannot share Communion with all of them, I can learn to love them as my brothers and sisters, and I can pray for the day when all divisions will end.

Despite my disappointment with the church's sins, despite my disillusionment with myself as a Christian and a leader, I remain grateful to belong to Jesus' family. And as I come to terms with our dysfunction, I begin to understand what it is to profess, as the ancient creeds do, "I *believe* in the church."[15] We are God's project, and we can be confident that he will finish what he started, even while it remains partially hidden from our view. This certain hope for the future animates how we live in the present: It enables us to keep showing up to each other and to him long after the stars have gone from our eyes.

And yet, this same hope also fuels our grief over the many ways we seem to resist God's work among us. To hope for restored relationships, repentance from sin, and renewal in the church is to know how far short we fall of these things.

Some of us have named grievances with Christian siblings in search of true peace and had our concerns dismissed as inordinate or imagined. Some of us have fought to stay in churches that pushed us out through their unwillingness to pursue truth or protect the vulnerable. Some of us have worked tirelessly for leadership reform, seeking to correct the abuses of the previous generation, only to witness a new expression of corruption take root during our tenure. Some of us have courageously called attention to problems in our midst, speaking out against patterns that are destroying us from the inside—and have been labeled as naysayers or saboteurs. Some of us struggle every Sunday to trust pastors or church leaders because of past hurts that were never acknowledged.

In the animated movie *Encanto*, a character named Bruno is estranged from his large, dynamic family. He is endowed with a supernatural gift—like all the members of this family—but his gift proved challenging for the rest of his family to receive. Bruno is a prophet, and some of his prophetic visions caused turmoil in the family. So Bruno disappears; at the start of the movie, one wonders if he is dead. Later on, we learn that Bruno has been living for years in the hidden passageways and attic of the family home. In one scene, we see a large dining table in the kitchen where all the members of the family are seated for a meal. On the other side of the wall, Bruno has pulled up a chair for himself, as if still seated at the family table though hidden from view.

I can't think of a better image for how many Christians experience their relationship with the church. Because of unacknowledged harm, unreconciled relationships, or unprocessed disillusionment, many of us live with a deep ambivalence about what it means to belong to God's family. As beautiful as the church is, it remains dysfunctional and broken. Sometimes the cognitive dissonance this creates is more than we can hold, so we self-exile—longing to share the family meal but choosing to stay hidden from view. Or we remain with the majority of the fellowship but live with a vague sense of regret about those estranged siblings who've come and gone from our sight.

At the end of *Encanto*, Bruno is restored to his family. They reconcile and rebuild their relationships with a renewed commitment to each other and to the grace from which their supernatural gifts have come. I believe the church's story will end like this too; one day, Jesus will gather up his broken body into one communion where all divisions are healed and all relationships are restored. On that day, we will feast at the longest table in the world, in the presence of peace himself.

Until then, we take and eat in anticipation.

In an ancient collection of church teachings called the *Didache*, there's a prayer that looks forward to this once-and-future unity of God's people: "As this broken bread was once scattered on the mountains, and after it had been brought together became one, so may thy church be gathered together from the ends of the earth unto thy kingdom; for thine is the glory, and the power, through Jesus Christ, forever."[16] For the first Christians, this prayer largely anticipated the evangelistic work of the church in calling all nations to follow Jesus as Lord. They knew the good news belonged to the whole world and their fellowship would one day reflect that.

But for modern Christians who have only ever known a fractured church, splintered by schism and fraught with corruption and conflict, this ancient prayer also speaks to a future reunification and healing for God's people.

Sometimes, when I celebrate the Lord's Supper, I think of those relationships in my own life that remain broken and seem unresolvable. I think of my father, whose death robbed him and others of greater reconciliation and wholeness in this life. I think of members in my family and my faith family, some of my closest Christian friends who cannot receive Communion from me or with me.[17] I think of people I know who love Jesus but have left the church or who are struggling to feel safe within it.

Presiding at this Table reminds me of the myriad ways we are not okay and don't know how to fix it. Then I break the bread, putting my trust again in the One who has allowed himself to be torn apart so that he might somehow put us back together.

7

ABUNDANCE

Will There Be Enough for Me?

---

*The bright shadow upon our outstretched hand, we know not
how, multiplies the bread and fish we offer, causes one woman's
spilt perfume to saturate millennia with its sweet fragrance, and
removes the cloaks of past miseries to reveal the blessings beneath.*

E. LILY YU, *BREAK, BLOW, BURN, AND MAKE*

MOST KIDS DON'T THINK ABOUT FINANCES. Or if they do,
their estimates are appropriately kid-sized. When we moved to a
new house last year, my sons guessed that we paid about $200 for it.

I wish they were right.

I didn't think much about money as a child, either. This was
primarily due to my family's privilege. My dad had a lucrative
career, and we always had more than we needed. Abundance was
built into our family culture, even well into my dad's illness. But
after he died, things changed. The specific causes of this are difficult
to map out in detail. My dad continued to work until he was too

physically sick to do so, but his job as an investment banker involved financial risk even under the best conditions. As cancer took hold of his mind and body, his business acumen progressively waned. In attempts to secure our future, he put his trust in some ventures that promised big returns but never came to fruition. Additionally, his family and personal health history meant he had not been able to secure life insurance before getting sick. These facts and factors all contributed to an unanticipated financial crisis with permanent consequences; about six weeks after he died, the bank foreclosed on our family home, and we had to move out.

Our home represented my dad's dream to see his family well provided for. It had everything he wanted for us: acres of outdoor space to roam, ample room to host friends and family, and—most importantly in my preteen estimation—enough bedrooms that I didn't have to share with either of my sisters.

Even though I was fourteen when it happened, I have almost no memories of packing up my room or saying goodbye to the home where my father took his last breaths. I do remember moving into the vacant Lutheran parsonage across town and the many people who helped us make it functional for a family of our size. These are good memories. The parsonage represented what (and who) we had lost, but it also represented God's profound care for us. What we hadn't sufficiently planned for or managed to preserve, God provided anyway.

I lived through high school in that borrowed house behind a church parking lot. By then I was old enough to pay a bit more attention to money. I was anxiously aware of grocery bills and the amount of food in our fridge—which, for a household with six kids, was often disappointing. I was also aware of the fact that my mom continued to tithe every dollar that passed through her hands. Her insistence on giving a percentage of our meager income to the church equally confounded and inspired me.

My response to these things was a mixed bag of faith and doubt. I was the recipient of provision that defied explanation; I knew we couldn't take credit for the clothes on our backs. But I also clung to those clothes with a primal fear that perhaps they, too, might be taken from me.

My family's cumulative experience of loss, and its material impact in the dramatic change to our financial situation, had its subtle effects in my life. My innate sentimentality rose to inordinate proportions, and I refused to throw anything away that carried memory or meaning to me. My natural thriftiness was animated by a deep-seated anxiety, compelling me to hoard packaged snacks or toiletry samples in case I needed them later. I never truly went without, but I lived with the semiconscious belief that I would, or at least that I might. This scarcity mentality has followed me into adulthood and even into ministry.

Poverty is more than a socioeconomic reality. It is also a frame of mind.

Usually, one precedes the other. The damaging effects of traumas like food insecurity are well-documented.[1] Children who grow up without enough to eat often can't escape their fear of hunger even after their situation changes. They may be compulsively frugal, perpetually stockpiling at the expense of present fullness. Or they might overindulge, seeking to make up for the memory of all those lost meals. I've heard stories illustrating both reactions from people who were born during the Great Depression, and similar ones from parents who've adopted children with difficult backgrounds. Scarcity is a specter that haunts our bodies, regardless of our age.

But fear of lack does not only stem from trauma. My children have never missed a meal in their lives, and yet my toddler intuitively double-fists her apple slices, keenly aware of her brothers' hovering presence. It seems that, to a degree, anxiety about having our needs met is built into our fallen human nature.

Oddly, this anxiety rarely disappears—even for those who live in prosperous nations and communities. We grow up with full bellies, but we fear missing out on the college scholarship, the job promotion, the right opportunities for our children. From an early age, we are trained to believe that in this world, there is not enough to go around. Not enough resources, not enough time, not enough wealth.

We learn to compete for these things—sometimes against others and sometimes against ourselves. We work hard to outshine our colleagues and obtain the coveted position at work. We race against the clock, irritated with ourselves for misplacing our car keys and wasting precious minutes of our day. Sometimes, our anxiety borders on the absurd and becomes a national story. For years after the Covid-19 lockdown, my local grocery store kept its ration-reminders visible on the shelves beside the price tag for popular items: "canned tuna—limit 4 per customer"; "toilet paper—limit 2 per customer."

Of course, there is truth to the scarcity myth. Shortages do happen. Resources are finite. We are finite. But when we respond to these realities by grasping more desperately for what we think we need, we perpetuate the problem we are trying to solve. We hoard what we have, afraid to share—and unwittingly contribute to the lack that others experience. We embrace hustle culture, conforming our bodies and minds to the kind of overwork that leads to burnout. This competitive, achievement-oriented striving characterizes America's "successful" economy. It also contributes to resource inequality and injustice on a global scale. When fear is our food, everyone goes hungry.

I first became aware of my relationship with scarcity in high school when I developed a habit of storing food away in various places. My purse always had something in it—usually a pack of peanut butter crackers, which for a season I considered a decent meal— but I also stashed snacks in my car glovebox, my trunk, and sometimes even my pocket. (I learned quickly that pockets don't make great lunch boxes.)

Today, as a mom of young children, I still almost always have food on my person. And I recognize that my teenage desire to keep snacks on hand was not a problem as much as the spirit behind it: I deeply feared being hungry and did not trust that food would always be provided for me. I anticipated that there would not be enough to pass around our family table and all be satisfied. So, I sought to make up the difference for myself, secretly—because I didn't want to share with my other hungry siblings.

This commitment eventually led me to hide food under my bed, which I remember doing quite carefully after being gifted a box of chocolates. I was so excited about this treat that I couldn't bring myself to eat it right away; I planned to ration it. But I knew if I stored it anywhere in my siblings' eyesight, someone would steal it. (To this day there are unsolved mysteries around who ate the hummus with my initials on the lid out of the fridge.) The problem with this plan was that I hid the chocolate so well I forgot about it. When I found it many months later, it was so dry and stale it had lost its appeal.

In the book of Exodus, God's people have a complicated relationship with food. After being rescued from slavery in Egypt, they
are journeying to a promised land "flowing with milk and honey"
when they realize they don't have enough food to hold them over
on the trip.[2] Instead of asking God to provide, they grumble against
their leaders and say they'd have been better off dying in Egypt,
where at least they had access to bread and meat. In response to
their grumbling, God provides bread that miraculously appears
each morning on the desert floor. Their instructions are to take as
much as they need for one day: "'Gather of it, each one of you, as
much as he can eat.' . . . Let no one leave any of it over till
the morning."

Of course, some of them don't follow this instruction. Rather
than trust that fresh bread will appear again each day, the newly
freed slaves try to stockpile this miracle food for future consumption. The hoarded bread, we learn, "bred worms and stank" by
the next morning.[3]

Old Testament scholar Walter Brueggemann describes the
exodus story as a clash of economies. In Egypt, Pharoah fears that
Joseph's descendants have become too numerous and might
overtake the Egyptians, so he enslaves them. He leads an economy
of competition, monopolizing the country's resources to exert
control over others. For generations, the Hebrews learn to live
under this regime. They are at the mercy of a merciless one, a pro-
vider who rations their food and murders their children.

But God's power proves greater than Pharoah's, and the Hebrews
walk free. They leave not penniless and naked from the shame of
slavery but dressed in the spoils of Egypt—silver and gold and
clothes freely given by the people who once enslaved them. Pharoah
even acknowledges God's superiority by asking Moses and Aaron

to bless him as they leave. Bruggemann comments, "The text shows that the power of the future is not in the hands of those who believe in scarcity and monopolize the world's resources; it is in the hands of those who trust God's abundance."[4]

After their dramatic vindication and rescue from Egypt, one might expect confidence—or at least gratitude—from the Hebrews. But their primary posture on the wilderness road is one of anxiety. They had suffered under Pharaoh for 430 years. Slavery was miserable, but at least it was familiar. At each point on the journey when they encounter uncertainty, they grumble. "It would have been better for us to serve the Egyptians than to die in the wilderness," they say.[5] There is a perverse comfort in choosing what we know, even if we know it isn't safe.

This, too, is a clash of economies. When we have grown up on a steady diet of scarcity, it takes time to trust abundance. This might be one explanation for the strange name God's people give the bread he sends them. Manna is a transliteration of the question they ask each other in Hebrew upon discovering it: *Man hu?* meaning "What is it?" When God answers their prayers, they don't recognize his provision. Bruggemann elaborates, "They had never before received bread as a free gift that they couldn't control, predict, plan for or own. The meaning of this strange narrative is that the gifts of life are indeed given by a generous God. It's a wonder, it's a miracle, it's an embarrassment, it's irrational, but God's abundance transcends the market economy."[6]

I would like to say that God's track record of provision in my life has healed my fear of scarcity over the years. But as my husband will attest, any financial uncertainty in our home is enough to start me stockpiling the peanut butter crackers again. (Sometimes, we laugh about this. Other times we fight about it.) When it comes to money, fear is my default posture. My body still believes that tragedy is around the corner.

Of course, real tragedy is unlikely: By global standards, I am quite wealthy. Even when my family spiraled after my dad's death, we were still relatively insulated. We might have been cash poor, but we remained resource-rich thanks to our community. On my more jaded days, I can reimagine God's miraculous provision during my teen years as simply another benefit of being from an affluent corner of the world. But what about the many people and families who don't have a wealthy network of friends nearby to offset a crisis? What about the children who are starving in countries around the world as I write this? What does it look like for them to trust God's abundance? Or is this only a promise for the privileged?

Ironically, the answer comes to me from the mouth of a poor woman whose own son would never purchase a home or live a financially secure life. When she discovered she was pregnant with the Messiah, Mary prophetically interpreted the clash of economies. In her famous Magnificat, she proclaimed, "[God] has filled the hungry with good things, and the rich he has sent away empty."[7] Even though Mary remained poor, and even though her son would grow up to be ravaged by those who hoarded power, Mary knew that God's generosity would ultimately triumph over every worldly monopoly. It was a promise she held by faith even before it had been fully born. Her body, pregnant with this promise, believed what her eyes had not yet seen.

I am learning, slowly, that trusting God's abundance is a prophetic act.

It requires faith—not that every bill will be paid and every meal provided in the short term but that these temporary outcomes have no say over our promised future. In the clash of economies, we are called to live by a currency that is still coming into the world. We are invited to feast on bread from heaven.

The only miracle of Jesus that is recorded in all four Gospels is his feeding of the five thousand.

Like the Hebrew slaves once did, a great multitude follows their prophet to a "desolate place" where food is nowhere to be found.[8] After a long day of Jesus' teaching, the disciples have a hungry crowd on their hands. Panic ensues. A little boy offers his five loaves of bread and two fish. Jesus gives his disciples a chance to partner with him in serving this meal, but they don't understand. They are still operating within the world's economy, where five loaves are irrelevant to the needs of five thousand people. By any human measure, there is no solution to the hunger before them. But Jesus takes, blesses, breaks, and gives the bread anyway.[9] After all eat and are satisfied, they collect twelve baskets of leftovers.

I once heard a preacher say about this story, "If you were good at math in school, you might struggle with the Bible." I have never been good at math. But I do like to have a handle on my resources so that I can carefully ration them. In his generosity, Jesus asks us to relinquish this perceived control so that he can do things we could never calculate on our own.

This miracle meal is also proof that Jesus cares for bodies as well as souls. He's not just showing off, he's feeding hungry people. But this act of kindness is not reducible to a formula for food on demand. In his own interpretation of the miracle, Jesus presses his listeners to seek not only "the food that perishes, but . . . the food that endures to eternal life."[10] The currency of the Kingdom is not less than a material resource; it is more than that. As Jesus points out, even those who ate the manna in the wilderness died eventually. But he has come so that those who feast on him will never die: "Whoever feeds on my flesh and drinks my blood has eternal life, and I will raise him up on the last day."[11]

In a world enslaved by scarcity, Jesus serves the one meal that will never run out. He nourishes us with his life. This doesn't automatically resolve our physical needs; trusting Jesus doesn't insulate us from hunger or hardship. It fills us with a different kind of fullness—a kind of life that transcends mere bodily existence even while securing our bodily future. And it heals us of our fearful striving for what we've never actually been able to secure on our own.

We might think we can provide for ourselves or our children through careful planning. We might think we can avoid rejection or harm through relational shrewdness. We might think we can remain insulated from failure through relentless perfectionism.

But beneath our hypervigilance, we remain dependent.

We are not enough.

In his ministry to the hungry crowd, Jesus demonstrates that our insufficiency is not the source of our shame; it is in fact the beginning of our healing. When we acknowledge our hunger, we learn to open our hands and receive. We learn to say with Mary, "He has filled the hungry with good things"—even before those good things have fully arrived.

Jesus, the Bread of Life, is the down payment on our future fullness. He has come and is coming into the world to renew it completely. We still wait for the day that was promised by the prophet Joel when "the threshing floors shall be full of grain; the vats shall overflow with wine and oil."[12] On that day, nobody will starve in a forgotten corner of the world; nobody will be ravaged by war or famine or poverty. Until then, we look to Jesus and realize that in him, that day is already dawning. As he feeds us, our bodies begin to believe the promise that with Jesus, there really is and always will be enough.

In college, I heard a missionary named Heidi Baker speak on poverty at the Princeton University Chapel. I had never heard of her before, and she was not what I expected given the setting: in the austere, gothic-style chapel of an Ivy League school, I anticipated a lecture on food insecurity and global inequity. When Heidi got up to speak, she started singing and waving her arms around. She was unconventional, but her message had a powerful impact on me. She spoke about working among some of the world's poorest children in Mozambique and how their profound need has allowed her to witness God's profound generosity. She was incredibly joyful. Her perspective and style are decidedly Pentecostal, but she shared one story that stoked my sacramental imagination as a burgeoning Anglican. I have revisited it many times in her writings:

> One night I was groaning in intercession for the children of Mozambique. . . . Then I had a dramatic, clear vision of Jesus. I was with him, and thousands and thousands of children surrounded us. I saw his shining face and his intense, burning eyes of love. I also saw his body. It was bruised and broken, and his side was pierced. He said, "Look into my eyes. You give them something to eat." Then he took a piece of his broken body and handed it to me. It became bread in my hands, and I began to give it to the children. It multiplied in my hands. Then again, the Lord said to me, "Look into my eyes. You give them something to drink." He gave me a cup of blood and water, which flowed from his side. I knew it was

a cup of suffering and joy. I drank it and then began to give it to the children to drink. The cup did not go dry. . . . The Lord spoke to my heart and said, "There will always be enough, because I died."[13]

This story speaks to my own memories as a child who wondered whether there would be enough for me. And it speaks to my ministry as a pastor, now that I frequently encounter others who are wondering the same thing. I don't regularly minister to people who are physically hungry. But every Sunday at church, I witness needs beyond my capacity to fill. As members of my congregation line up to receive Communion, I see people who are struggling in their marriages, who are wrestling with doubts, who are haunted by childhood traumas. In my limitations as a minister and as a human, I can't come close to resolving these issues. Even the needs of my own three children overwhelm me.

Sometimes, I try to suppress this fact.

I trick myself into thinking I can be the provision others need. I attempt to be smart enough, compelling enough, compassionate enough to satisfy their hunger. In doing this, however, I realize that I am actually looking to *them* for provision—hoping to feed my fragile ego through a feeling of sufficiency. Even heroism can be a form of bondage to scarcity: I fear not being seen, or not being seen as good enough, so I compete for a place of honor and importance in their lives. As one of six children competing to be seen by a finite father and mother, I internalized this particular lie well before my dad ever got sick.

But at the Lord's Table, I remember that my hunger to be seen and to be fed has already been provided for. I don't need to be enough in myself, because he is enough for us all. The more I practice receiving this, the more comfortable I am acknowledging my gratitude. And the more confident I am that the same grace on offer today will be available tomorrow, even if (and when) I fail to recognize it at first.

When we've been raised on a scarcity diet, it takes time to trust abundance. It takes time to recognize the sensation of fullness. But when we do, we stop grasping for what we think we need, and we start offering up what we actually have. Our resources are inadequate: pitiful loaves before a hungry crowd. Our intelligence, our creativity, our bank accounts will never be sufficient to address the multitude of complexity and need in front of us. But when we relinquish control and offer our gifts to God, he multiplies them—to his glory, not our own.

This does not make the offering painless.

Letting go will always involve some risk, some death to the comfort of self-sufficiency. I am still tempted to hoard my resources, either because I want to enjoy them for myself or because I don't want to be exposed as not having enough. I don't want to come to the end of my pantry shelves or the end of myself. But as Jesus told us and later showed us, "Unless a grain of wheat falls into the earth and dies, it remains alone; but if it dies, it bears much fruit."[14]

The economy of the Kingdom, then, is eucharistic: We stretch out our hands, we break, we give ourselves away, and we observe the mysterious multiplication of grace. When we are willing to find ourselves lacking we will also find him there, ready to feed us all.

8

HOSPITALITY

The Fullness That Feeds Others

The world today is hungry not only for bread but hungry for love; hungry to be wanted, to be loved. They're hungry to feel that presence of Christ. In many countries, people have everything except that presence, that understanding. That's why the life of prayer and sacrifice comes to give that love. Through your dedication, you are to be that presence, that bread of God to break.

MOTHER TERESA, *JESUS, THE WORD TO BE SPOKEN*

THE NIGHT BEFORE I FOUND OUT I was pregnant with our firstborn, I dreamed of my dad.

As dreams sometimes go, there wasn't much of a plotline. But it was a vivid scene in which we sat across from each other at a restaurant table. Between us was an enormous spread of food. All my favorite entrees were there, including what would become my telltale pregnancy craving: fried chicken. In the dream, I understood that he'd taken me out for a special meal. I woke with a vague sense of blessing and provision.

As the day went on, I didn't make much of the dream. But late that afternoon, I was goaded into taking a pregnancy test by some friends—my husband and I were not trying to conceive, so I wasn't particularly expectant—and when the test read positive, I immediately remembered my dad sitting across the table from me, smiling. In the months leading up to this day, I had grown quite nervous about getting pregnant because I feared all the unknowns: How will we pay our bills? How will this impact my work? Will I be a good mom? My scarcity mindset stalked our vision for family life. Into this anxiety, my dream spoke with God's voice: *"Don't worry, I will provide. I will nourish and bless you as you begin this assignment."*

When we've spent years recovering from deficits, it's natural to avoid new ones. We've worked hard for stasis; we don't want to disrupt it. But the Christian life is about more than recovery. We are called to ministry. Sometimes, this call is placed upon us before we feel entirely ready. For me, motherhood was such a call. But it came in a way that convinced me: With the call comes the capacity. Through us, God can and will feed others.

The first time I was called to ministry, I needed no reassurance. I was eight.

Like many young Baptists (at least, the nerdy homeschooled ones), I grew up reading missionary biographies. Gladys Aylward, Lottie Moon, and Amy Carmichael were some of my childhood heroes. These women were brave and unrelenting in their commitment to share God's love with people they'd never met. I aspired to be like them. And I assumed, given my church context, that this meant I would grow up to be a crosscultural missionary.

Though I dabbled with other age-appropriate career goals during my elementary years (marine biologist, professional artist, and the generic but alluring "singer" all captivated me at various points), my underlying desire to work for God never dissipated. In sixth grade, when my mom transitioned to full-time caregiving for my dad and could no longer homeschool us, I began attending a local school. At the end of the year, each student got to publish their vocational aspirations beneath their yearbook photo. Mine read "Missionary for Christ." (It was a Christian school, so I was not teased too badly for this.)

Over time, however, the gap between my aspirations and my lifestyle widened considerably. As childhood idealism gave way to adolescent grief, I medicated the pain of my dad's death in the only ways I knew how. I experimented with behaviors that I was told might give me some relief or that at least would identify me as the "troubled teenager" I felt I was becoming. Those behaviors achieved the latter but not the former. By the middle of high school, I was seen not as the pious future missionary I once thought myself to be but as a classic case of what happens when a family falls apart.

Though I wanted to be understood and helped, I deeply resented my reputation as an example of "fatherlessness"—largely because it added to the shame I already felt over our loss. In the affluent evangelical subculture where I grew up, there was an unspoken stigma attached to family instability. My situation no longer fit the requisite mold for a model Christian student. And my interior life seemed to confirm others' perception: I felt as broken as I must have looked. So, the experimental behaviors continued. They continued to disappoint. And I continued to feel a call to ministry—a desire to offer my life to God in some way—but I didn't know how to reconcile that story with the one I was living.

These disparate parts of myself were gathered up and integrated through the patient ministry of adult mentors. They taught me not to see myself through the lens of Christian stereotypes, but through the eyes of God. All his children, whether or not they aspire to be missionaries, are troubled and in trouble. Some of our histories may be more colorful than others, but all of them must be washed clean by Jesus' blood.

These trusted adults walked me through the basics of the gospel in real time, until grace became more than a theological concept; it became my lived experience. When I look back on those years, I think of David's famous proclamation from Psalm 23: "You prepare a table before me in the presence of my enemies." While assaulted by shame from without and within, God nourished and protected me. He fed me spiritually while I grieved the death of my earthly father and learned how to belong to my heavenly one.

Jesus' longest parable, commonly called "the prodigal son," begins and ends with a generous father. The story starts with the younger of two sons asking what would have been a disgraceful question in his cultural context: He requests his portion of the family inheritance up front, as if to say, "I'm tired of waiting around for you to die." Shockingly, the father grants this request. After the younger son leaves his family and squanders his inheritance, he returns home to beg for a place among his father's servants. But before he has the chance to say anything, his father kisses and clothes him and calls for a feast to celebrate his son's return. The older son, who had remained dutiful and obedient at home, chafes against this lavish display of affection for the prodigal. But again, the father responds with inordinate generosity. He pleads with his older son to join the celebration and insists, "all that is mine is yours."[1]

Like many Christians who read this story, I see myself in both sons. As a hurting teenager, I willfully rebelled against the God I loved; but his unwavering embrace healed the shame of my home-coming. And as a self-identified "future missionary," I once felt proud of my obedience—and was surprised to discover that none of what God had given me was earned. He gives from the pleasure of his love, not from the compulsion of our deserving. Each one of us, regardless of our title or our track record, is the recipient of his profound hospitality.

The eucharistic feast at the center of our worship allows us to rehearse this truth regularly. When we come to the Lord's Supper, we remember that we are welcomed and wanted at God's table as we are. "All that is mine is yours," he says to us as he offers up his life for ours. In responding to this invitation, we encounter what Henri Nouwen described as "the love that existed before any rejection was possible and that will still be there after all rejections have taken place."[2] This encounter is the foundation of all authentic ministry. It is the meal in which our Father sits across from us smiling as he provides the needed sustenance for all future assignments. From the fullness we find there, we learn to feed others.

Christianity is unique among religions in that it *begins* with home-coming. God's welcome is not only a finish line (though we do anticipate it at the end of life); it is a starting point. Before we earn or achieve anything, we are called daughters and sons. Our fundamental posture is that of reception and response to God's initiative. But as Paul pointed out in his letter to the Romans, if we are God's children, we are also his heirs.[3] Having experienced his radical hospitality, we become those who offer it ourselves. We grow up into the image of our Father.

In his poignant book *The Return of the Prodigal Son*, Nouwen reflects on this realization in his own life:

For a long time I have lived with the insight that returning to my Father's home was the ultimate call. It has taken me much spiritual work to make the elder son as well as the younger son in me turn around and receive the welcoming love of the Father. The fact is, on many levels, I am still returning. But the closer I come to home the clearer becomes the realization that there is a call beyond the call to return. It is the call to become the father who welcomes home and calls for a celebration. Having reclaimed my sonship, I now have to claim fatherhood. . . . I now see that the hands that forgive, console, heal, and offer a festive meal must become my own.[4]

In my spiritual journey, nothing has been more transformative than reclaiming my identity as a daughter. Childhood loss shaped my self-understanding as that of an outsider; I was the one without a father, without a proper home, without a sense of my belovedness in the world. Through the Eucharist, I've come home to the Father who calls me his own. I belong at his Table. It has been the great surprise of my life, then, to discover my call to now stand on the other side of that Table and extend the same belonging to others. When I serve Communion, I have the privilege of welcoming sons and daughters home. It is the missionary work I didn't know to aspire to but that I now understand as the fulfillment of my childhood dream—because it is the overflow of God's mission to me.

Not everyone is called to be a priest who offers the Eucharist. But every Christian is called to the eucharistic ministry of hospitality. We are welcomed by Christ, and then recruited to extend that welcome to others. We are nourished by Christ, and then sent out to nourish the world in his strength. This is why in some Christian traditions, church is called mass, which comes from the same linguistic root as the word *mission*: Our worship around the Lord's Table is the beginning of our ministry to the world. In the Anglican church, every Sunday service ends with a charge: "Go in peace to love and serve the Lord."

Thinking of our mission in eucharistic terms protects us from the triumphalism that has so often sullied Christian witness; it reminds us that the gospel is not an ultimatum as much as it is an invitation. "Christian mission is not about conquering, winning, or even changing the world," writes Ed Smither. "Rather, mission is a joyfully relational endeavor of crossing boundaries between the already and not yet people of God."[5] We move toward the world as witnesses of Isaiah's prophetic vision that God is preparing "a feast of rich food" for all peoples.[6] As those who feast on Christ, we know this promise is coming true.

Our communion with Jesus does not erase every ache; we feast in anticipation of the fullness to come. But in the meantime, he does fill us enough to have something to give others. In responding to his call, we minister with his resources. We become teachers of what we ourselves once lacked. And in the mystery of hospitality, we discover that when we are willing to become hosts of God's presence—when we offer welcome and nourishment to others in his name—we end up being the guests of God's gracious visitation. In giving, we receive. In living as the Father, we become truer sons. By doing as he does, we grow up into his image.

When we participate in God's hospitality, grace blurs the line between host and guest. This, too, protects us from triumphalism. It reminds us that even when we offer care or welcome, we are never unilateral power-holders. Instead, as Miroslav Volf has pointed out, we are "simultaneously receivers and givers."[7]

This has always been the case. In Genesis 18, Abraham is sitting in his tent when three mysterious travelers show up, hungry and vulnerable in the desert sun. Abraham runs out to meet them, like the father in Luke's parable who greets his prodigal child. The model host, Abraham welcomes and feeds these visitors at great cost and great risk to himself. While they eat in the shade of the trees, they tell Abraham that his wife Sarah will have a son within a year's time. At ninety years old, the still-childless Sarah laughs when she overhears this news. She had offered the visitors what she had faith for: a nourishing meal in the heat of the day. In return, they offered her something beyond her ability to imagine.

Christian interpretation of this story has identified Abraham's mysterious visitors as somehow a manifestation of God. Andrei Rublev's famous icon *The Trinity* depicts them as three angelic beings seated around a table in an open circle of fellowship. The viewer of the icon is seemingly invited to pull up a chair and sit with these divine visitors. Like Abraham, we can become God's guests, God's friends. But the biblical story reminds us that this blessing came in response to *Abraham's* act of hospitality. In welcoming the stranger, Abraham was welcomed. In taking the risk of becoming the host, he was surprised to become the guest.

As a pastor, and in my own life, I have noticed the tendency to avoid the risk of welcoming others for fear of not being adequately equipped. Most of us are still working on our own recovery, seeking our own nourishment. We assume we don't have anything to give until we are fully satiated. There is wisdom in discerning our capacity to give and pacing our participation with others while we heal. But to a degree, our healing also comes through the exercise of self-giving, because only then do we recover our purpose as conduits of grace and not merely recipients.

Miroslav Volf elaborates: "We were created to be and to act like God. And so the flow of God's gifts shouldn't stop as soon as it reaches us. The outbound movement must continue. Indeed, in addition to making us flourish, giving to others is the very purpose for which God gave us the gifts."[8]

One reason I feared becoming a mom was because I felt, subconsciously, that my own development as a daughter had been interrupted. How could I offer to a child what I still hungered to receive? But as I've grown into my ministry as a mother, I've realized that in parenting my children, God is parenting me. He has supplied me with a love I thought I was still looking for—and in giving it away, I am finding it for myself. My delight for my children helps me understand God's delight for me. I see them, and I know that in some way, I am seen. I am God's child.

If I had waited until I felt ready to become a mom, I might still be waiting. But in accepting the call, I am growing into it. In becoming food for my children, I am being fed.

In his commitment to hospitality, God has dignified the role of guest as well as host by assuming them both. Christine Pohl observes:

> Writers in the New Testament portray Jesus as a gracious host, welcoming children and prostitutes, tax collectors and sinners into his presence. . . . But Jesus, God incarnate, is also portrayed as a vulnerable guest and needy stranger, one who "came to his own home" and often received no welcome (John 1:11). In his life on earth, Jesus experienced the vulnerability of the homeless infant, the child refugee, the adult with no place to lay his head, the despised convict.[9]

As a human being, Jesus identifies with every hungry, lonely person in the world. In the first few centuries of the church, this truth gave birth to a uniquely Christian ministry of hospitality to the poor. Mother Teresa is perhaps the most famous example of this ministry in recent history. She devoted her life to serving the poorest of the poor in Calcutta, India. As a Christian missionary, she saw an organic relationship between her devotion to Jesus and her devotion to the people who suffered on the streets. And as a Roman Catholic, she saw a similar relationship between Christ's presence in the Eucharist and his presence in those suffering people. She is known to have said, "In the mass we have Jesus in the appearance of bread, while in the slums I see Christ in the distressing disguise of the poor. The Eucharist and the poor are but one love for me."[10]

But Mother Teresa's observation about the Eucharist reveals another aspect of God's hospitality: In Christ, God became not only the host and the guest but also the meal. Jesus gave his life to be broken and poured out on the cross so that we might live. The story behind the Supper reminds us that Jesus did not merely pay the cost of our welcome and nourishment; he became our nourishment himself.

As Christians, we never seek to replicate or replace Jesus' sufficient gift. But we are called to be conformed to it. In his letter to the Romans, Paul urges us to present our bodies as "living sacrifices."[11] Our self-donation can't forgive someone's sins or satisfy their spiritual hunger; but it can become the means through which God manifests *his* life to them. We offer ourselves to the Father, and then he makes us an offering for others. In this way, our lives become eucharistic—signs of God's presence and provision in the world.

Sometimes we see the fruit of this ministry, sometimes we don't. My dad didn't. As a fearful father with an unknown future, he offered his cancer to God. He didn't live to witness how that act of submission has fed me over these many years. Shortly after his diagnosis, he copied a section of Oswald Chambers's *My Utmost for His Highest* in his journal:

> We have to exercise ourselves in order that the Son of God may be manifested in our mortal flesh. . . . Our Lord never dictated to His Father, and we are not here to dictate to God; we are here to submit to His will so that He may work through us what He wants. When we realize this, He will make us broken bread and poured-out wine to feed and nourish others.[12]

The ultimate act of hospitality is to allow ourselves to become, in God's hands, bread for breaking.

I used to think the ministry of broken bread—of a life that nourishes others—was reserved for those who had already mastered basic Christianity, those "honor roll" Christians whom God would be proud to present to the world as an example of himself. This is why, during my youthful dysfunction, I assumed I was disqualified. But in paying attention to the people God has given to me for nourishment, I have realized this is a fallacy. In fact, the people who have shaped my faith most profoundly are the ones who've allowed me to see the truth about their deepest fears and failures. Their willingness to open their lives as examples not of their obedience but of God's mercy was a kind of hospitality that helped me feel at home in my own experience of faith.

One of my best friends is following Jesus in a difficult season of celibacy. Her faithfulness to this call is commendable, but she doesn't wear it like an accomplishment. She is honest about her desperation for help. Her ability to admit struggle and to ask for

God's strength to uphold her encourages me as much as her commitment to chastity. She is not afraid to be seen as she is: a broken human being in need of grace. When my sister went through a difficult, future-defining season of her own, this friend of mine met with her regularly to talk and pray. I remember my sister saying after one of their talks, "I've never met anyone who loves Jesus that much."

Our imperfections aren't a barrier to ministry; they are a pathway.

We offer ourselves as we are—sinful, weak, in recovery, in the middle of stories we are ashamed of—so that God's healing in us can become a source of healing for others. Henri Nouwen, whose own ministry was a beautiful example of this in its generous vulnerability, wrote, "Laying down your life means making your own faith and doubt, hope and despair, joy and sadness, courage and fear available to others as ways of getting in touch with the Lord of life."[13]

This is not the same thing as making peace with dysfunction or operating from woundedness in the name of ministry. Apart from active submission to God, we will more likely be wounded wounders than wounded healers.[14] Sometimes, being a living sacrifice means stepping back from activities or opportunities that we aren't healthy enough to handle appropriately. But even this, in its self-offering, can become eucharistic and therefore a source of nourishment for others. It illustrates how, in view of God's mercy, we can learn to relinquish all things and entrust ourselves to the One who alone can restore us. Then, in his way and in his timing, our wounds are transfigured as scars—still telling the truth about our injuries but now safe for others to touch.

Into my twenties, my arms bore little white scars from some of the experimental behaviors I'd tried as a young teenager. I learned not to be ashamed of them, but instead to see them as evidence of God's healing work in me. He preserved me during those years of self-hatred and self-harm and taught me, slowly, how to live as someone who is loved. Over the decades, those scars have faded from view. But as my friend Robert recently observed, the deepest wounds in our lives happen "in the mysterious intersection of the material and physical. These wounds may or may not leave a physical scar in their wake, but at a deeper level, they leave a scar on our soul, pains and aches that linger and often seem beyond remedy."[15]

I don't believe the scars of losing my dad will ever fully fade from my soul. And I no longer believe this is a liability. Their lingering ache teaches me to live in closer proximity to the Healer, and it gives me greater tenderness toward the wounds of others. In this way, my ongoing experience of need is simultaneously the greatest gift I have to give.

This is true for every Christian. We don't minister as those who've already been perfected, but as those who bear witness to the perfect love available to us all. As we continue to come to him, we grow confident enough to go out to others to share what we've received. We learn to say to our friends, our children, our neighbors, "Here is my life: Here are my failures and my fragility, here is God's mercy. Take and eat."

9

COURAGE

When Self-Giving Includes Loss

"Real isn't how you are made," said the Skin Horse.
"It's a thing that happens to you. . . ."
"Does it hurt?" asked the Rabbit.
"Sometimes," said the Skin Horse, for he was always truthful.
"When you are Real you don't mind being hurt."

MARGERY WILLIAMS, *THE VELVETEEN RABBIT*

EARLY ON THANKSGIVING MORNING 2018, I woke up to a text from my sister Miriam. "Can you talk?" she asked.

My husband and I were living in Northern Virginia at the time, and this was the first Thanksgiving in years that we wouldn't be joining the rest of my family at my grandfather's house in Georgia. We had been gathering there for the holiday since the year my father died.

I assumed my sister probably just wanted to chat since we wouldn't be together later in the day, so I responded casually. "Sure! Call you in a few."

Her next message surprised me: "No kids in the room, please."

My toddler and infant sons were already downstairs with my husband, so I shut the bedroom door and called right away.

"Are you sitting down?" She asked me after answering the phone.

I don't remember anything she said in detail after that. Only that after our short conversation, I knew my youngest brother was dead.

In recounting the events that shaped my childhood, I've not mentioned my five siblings much. This is intentional—their stories are not mine to tell. Our loss might have been public, but each of us has the right to steward the personal details of our response. It is also worth saying that our accounts of growing up are all slightly different. Our memories and interpretations of our family's story bear similarities, but also distinctions. Six children represent six unique perspectives.

One of my deepest adult griefs is that my brother Noah isn't here anymore to articulate his perspective. He's not here to tell us why he decided, in the middle of the night, less than a month after his twenty-first birthday, to take his own life.

In the weeks after he died, my mom and siblings and I tried desperately to string together a narrative of his last week on earth. He did not leave a note explaining his decision or even saying goodbye. In the absence of information, we theorized. We pored over his journals, dissected our last conversations with him, spoke at length with the officers who'd found him. Of course, nothing we discovered eased our bewilderment and confusion about his death. What I've since learned about suicide grief (and, by extension, all grief) is that explanations aren't the same as answers. Even if someone leaves a note before leaving the world, those left behind will still have a thousand unanswerable questions.

Noah was nine years younger than me, which means most of my memories of him are from when he was a child. I left for college when he was nine. I began getting to know him as an adult when he lived with my husband and me in Virginia one summer, about a year before he died. Every day he would bike five miles from our house to the train station, take the train into Washington, DC, pull tourists around in a pedicab until late afternoon, then bike back home from the train station. Upon returning to our house, he'd sit on the kitchen counter with his feet up, balancing ice packs on both his knees. He consumed an amount of calories I did not know was possible. He adored my sons. He read a lot. And he shared with me, in fits and starts, some of what animated his interior life.

Noah had always been a serious child. When my dad died, he was only five—but he stood by the open casket, immovable, throughout the wake before the funeral. As he studied and stroked my father's inanimate face, he asked repeatedly, "Why is he so cold?" None of us could provide an answer to his satisfaction.

My siblings and I thought, or hoped, that Noah would find his way through adolescence. We'd all had our challenges growing up, and he did too. We believed for him.

The summer Noah spent in my home deepened my own belief that he was going to be okay. And it deepened my love for him. After he moved out, he lived nearby in Washington, DC, for a while, which meant he would still occasionally come over for a visit and a free meal. (His caloric needs remained impressive.) One night after leaving our house, I reminded him that our guest room was still available if he ever needed it.

"Thanks," he responded. "Your house feels like home."

The following spring, he stayed with us the night before embarking on a solo cross-country bicycle trip. As he prepared to leave, I discovered that he was planning to bike from Virginia to

South Carolina—without a helmet. I gave him mine, plus a handful of granola bars. We took a picture together then said goodbye. It was the last time he ever spoke to me.

As much as I may want to, I can't know the mind of my brother or presume to give an account for his life. His story is his own, now sealed and waiting to be told by the only One who knows its true meaning. "Within limits we can know," wrote Wendell Berry; "within somewhat wider limits we can imagine. We can extend compassion to the limit of imagination. We can love, it seems, beyond imagining. But how little we can understand!"[1]

I didn't understand why, of all the years, my husband and I had chosen not to go to Georgia that Thanksgiving. Most of my family was together when they heard about Noah's death while we were eight hundred miles north. But days later, when my mom and every one of my siblings made the trip to Virginia to identify Noah's body with me, I did come to understand my purpose in having remained. Noah had died just across the state line in Maryland. My house would become home base—not for a reunion, but for a goodbye.

After getting to know Noah as an adult, I hoped to be the person he would call upon periodically to feed him and make sure his bike helmet was still in good condition. Instead, I would be the one to sign his death certificate and drive his ashes across the country to his memorial service. I wanted my love to look a certain way in his life. It ended up looking quite different.

In losing my brother, I've begun to realize that where understanding and even imagination fall short, love remains. But in standing apart from these things, love doesn't always look the way we want it to. It calls us to give of ourselves without assurances of outcomes. In the absence of understanding, love requires courage.

Before my brother moved in with us, my husband and I rented a room of our house to an international student from South Korea. He had great fun pointing out cultural differences between us and describing his non-Western sensibilities. Often when I asked him if he liked a certain book or movie, he'd laugh and say, "well, it's very American." What he meant by this, I learned, is that American stories are predictably optimistic: the guy will get the girl, the hero will be vindicated, the ending will be happy. There are exceptions to this, but they only prove the overall trend.

American evangelicals have our own version of "happily-ever-after" thinking. We assume that because Jesus was raised from the dead, love always wins. When people encounter this love, they will be healed and made whole. We tend to believe that because the gospel is true, it "works" in people's lives. As evidence for this belief, Christians often emphasize stories of redemption. We love testimonies about the addict who finds sobriety, the adopted child who embraces a new home, the broken marriage that is restored.

These stories are worth emphasizing, of course. They illustrate God's resurrection power and remind us of what is possible. But in our religious optimism, we sometimes pressurize these stories into an artificial simplicity. We presume that God's grace, rightly applied, *always* produces these kinds of results—that if we just love people enough, we will have something to show for it.

I took some of these presumptions into ministry with me. My college years bore witness to profound transformation in people's lives. And the church I served after seminary was emphatic that God's love can change the world. I encouraged others to share this love with their colleagues and neighbors, confident of the outcomes they could expect.

But then my brother killed himself—three weeks before my ordination as a priest. His death called my paradigm for ministry into question: If the gospel works, why hadn't it worked for him? Can love really heal people, or is it just a nice sentiment for the psycho-logically secure? In the weeks leading up to my ordination, I was haunted by these questions. I wondered how to avoid making false promises to the people I would lead as a priest. I wondered what I could confidently say to them about the hope we hold for ourselves and others—about whether Jesus' resurrection makes any dif-ference in the face of mental illness and childhood trauma and generational brokenness. As my ordination approached, I asked myself: *If love doesn't guarantee results, what does it do, exactly?*

My first Sunday back in church after my brother died was jarring. Usually, I adored the exuberant worship that my congregation was known for. Our morning services opened with organ music and a robed choir but also included a contemporary praise band with three guitars and a full drum kit. On any given week I could expect to see someone dancing in the back row or an elderly church ma-triarch shaking a tambourine near the front. We represented a joyful mix of styles and sensibilities and a love for singing.

But three days after learning of my brother's suicide, I felt pain-fully out of place among this cheerful group. I didn't know how to sing along with songs about God's victory over darkness or our joy in salvation. I still believed these things to be factually true, but their jubilant tone was utterly dissonant with my current emotional landscape. I sat there, motionless, carried by the worship of others.

Then the time came for Communion. The mood in the room changed to one of quiet reverence. Our pastor stood behind the enormous wooden table at the front of the sanctuary, upon which sat bread and wine. As he began to tell the story of the Last Supper, I heard the familiar words as if for the first time: "On the night he was betrayed . . ."

There, in the center of our worship, I felt comforted by the most un-American story ever told. Our hero's life did not end in vindication and victory but in betrayal and abandonment. Jesus was the perfect expression of God's love in the world, and the only result he had to show for it was his own blood on the ground. I'd never thought deeply about the fact that on their last night together, Jesus served the Passover meal to his friends knowing that they would all turn away from him. He said to Judas, "This is my body, given for you," knowing he would sell him to his murderers. He washed Peter's feet, knowing Peter would deny him.

For Jesus, love was never about returns or results. It was a gift that he gave even though he knew it would be misunderstood and rejected. His obedience and his confidence did not hinge on others' responses. He knew who he was and what he had come to do. He gave this gift unto death.

Of course, in his resurrection, Jesus *was* ultimately vindicated. And his gift did not return void, for his friends were restored to him—as many as were willing to receive mercy and forgiveness.[2] Jesus' resurrection is proof that love is not impotent, even if we can't see its intended effects in the short term.

But in view of my brother's death, I realized how often I had rushed to the resurrection without internalizing the significance of what led up to it. In real time, Jesus' ministry *seemed* to have been a failure. As he hung on the cross, love looked more like losing than like winning. Although Jesus knew his future victory was secure, he still submitted himself to the humiliation of apparent defeat. He still endured the existential angst of abandonment by his friends and followers, the people he loved to the end.[3]

Jesus' passion makes it clear: The gospel does "work"—but not always in the way we like to imagine. God doesn't promise to tie up every story with a neat bow of redemption, at least not in this life. He didn't for Jesus. Sometimes our stories will seem to end in failure. Sometimes our love seems to return void. This should not surprise us. Nor should it deter us from continuing to believe that God's promises are true. Rather, it should give us courage to stay the path of love, regardless of temporary outcomes.

Three weeks after that first Sunday without my brother, I stood behind the same enormous Communion table at my church to celebrate the Eucharist for the first time. Tears spilled from my eyes as I offered the bread to my congregation. Though still wracked with grief and confusion, I also felt a new, deep-seated clarity as I told the story of Jesus' self-giving love. He was willing to be rejected for us; we don't need to be afraid of being rejected for him.

Although we know from Scripture that the Last Supper was foundational to the institution and meaning of the Eucharist,[4] Christians didn't consistently mention it in their eucharistic liturgies until the fourth century.[5] Historians speculate about why it came to be included at that time. One theory is that as the church grew, so did the need for *catechesis*—teaching about the faith. Worship services were a natural time to add more teaching, so eucharistic prayers grew longer and more explanatory; mentioning the Last Supper each week before sharing Communion ensured that everyone present could hear and understand the meaning behind this sacred meal.

The addition of what's commonly called "the institution narrative" into the Sunday liturgy (Jesus' instruction to his disciples to "do this in remembrance of me") might also have been related to the cessation of martyrdom. In the first three centuries of the church, Christians were persecuted. They intuitively understood that following Jesus included the possibility of dying like him. "In the age of the martyrs," explains Paul Bradshaw, "Christians hardly needed reminding that sharing in 'the cup of Christ,' the supreme Martyr himself, brought precisely the possibility of sharing in the number of the martyrs, just as their baptism also implied."⁶

But with the end of persecution and the legalization of Christianity, this possibility faded from Christian consciousness. It became essential to remind churchgoers that the Lord's Supper necessarily incorporates his *Last* Supper—that Jesus' ministry to us was unto death. As his followers, our ministry to others might well be the same.

For me, a modern Christian living in the Bible Belt of the American South, martyrdom remains an unlikely prospect. But I still need to be reminded that Jesus' love for humanity was met with betrayal and abandonment—because it protects me from idealizing the life he calls me to live. In my optimism, I want to believe that if I love others like Jesus loves them, they will come to love him—and me—in return. If I parent my children well enough, they will grow up to follow Jesus and thank me for being such a great mom. If I authentically care for members of my congregation, they will find their way to spiritual maturity and health and be faithful leaders in the church. If I represent my faith with intelligence and respect, my ideological neighbors will be won over, or at least they will think well of me.

But this is not how it worked for Jesus.

He didn't measure the quality of his love against the favorability of others' responses. He gave himself with no strings attached. His example reminds me that the Christian life is about obedience, not outcomes. We are called to a *cruciform*—a cross-shaped—love that may not result in people reciprocating, appreciating, or even acknowledging us at all. Instead, it may result in persistent rejection and ridicule.

In his ministry as the Roman Catholic archbishop of El Salvador, Oscar Romero sought to embody this love for the people of his country. Appointed during a time of political violence and civil unrest, Romero took a stand against the corrupt government regime as well as against the various guerilla groups that rose up in response. In his sermons, he condemned violence but also offered grace. He often directly addressed any military members who might be listening over the radio, extending God's love and for-giveness to them for their crimes against the poor.

In response to his unpopular message, Romero was murdered while preparing to celebrate the Eucharist at a church service. As he lay dying, his last words were, "May God have mercy on the assassins."[7]

Sometimes, for reasons we can't know, people refuse the mercy that is offered to them. But Romero's witness reminds me that their rejection doesn't diminish the offering; if anything, it makes the offering more powerful. Unrequited kindness is never wasted. In-stead, it is a seed that dies, planted in the soil of a kingdom that remains hidden. We may not see its fruit now, but one day we will sit together under its shade and remember.

In the weeks after my brother died, my kids watched a lot of TV. They were young enough to not know what their options were, so they were happy watching endless reruns of *Mister Rogers' Neigh-borhood.* It was the only show quiet enough for my raw nerves.

One afternoon I was zoned out on the sofa next to my toddler when Daniel Tiger, a ratty puppet whose voice belongs to Fred Rogers, started singing. "Sometimes I wonder if I'm a mistake," he began. I listened as Daniel named his insecurities and questioned his worth in the presence of his friend Lady Aberlin. Aberlin, an actress and singer who played herself on the show, responded with a song of her own when Daniel finished. She started with, "I like you just the way that you are, I really do like you."

When she finished, Daniel didn't react; he simply started re-peating his original tune. "Sometimes I wonder if I'm a mistake," he began again. The two sang in tandem now, each reiterating their original message to the other. The song ended without resolution, without a clear winner. I still think of this duet often.

And I still sometimes wish I knew what my brother had heard in response to his own self-doubt, what voices or melodies filled his mind when he allowed himself to wonder. It seemed that, for whatever reason, shame had sung to him the loudest in the end. This grieves me. And it angers me to think that there were people and situations in his life that amplified the shame he felt. This, too, is for God alone to know and address.

But in my grief, I also feel profound gratitude for the many people who lent their voices to tell Noah, truthfully, "I really do like you." Throughout his life, there was a refrain of love and welcome and, if not understanding, acceptance of him always playing in the background. My whole family contributed to it, though imperfectly, along with many others, whose involvement in Noah's life I did not discover until he died: childhood Sunday school teachers and dads of his friends and friends of our family who liked Noah and wanted him around and wanted him to believe that.

To love someone is really to be powerless. It's to sing a refrain the other person may not be able to hear. To love is to embrace the possibility of rejection and loss.

But however our individual duets sound to our ears, our choice to sing forever changes the nature of the song. Everyone who loved Noah added beauty and texture to his life and prevented him from singing alone. That is something we will never regret.

In *The Four Loves*, C. S. Lewis challenges, "with trembling," an argument that St. Augustine made in his *Confessions*. After the pain of losing a dear friend, Augustine suggests that it is better to only love God, since only God will never pass away. Lewis agrees that it is certainly safer to avoid entanglements that can wound us. "Of course this is excellent sense. . . . Of all arguments against love none makes so strong an appeal to my nature as 'Careful! This might lead you to suffering.'"[8]

But then he questions whether such precautions, appealing as they are, are appropriately Christian: "We follow One who wept over Jerusalem and at the grave of Lazarus," he points out. And "Even if it were granted that insurances against heartbreak were our highest wisdom, does God Himself offer them? Apparently not. Christ comes at last to say, 'Why hast thou forsaken me?'"[9]

God, it seems, did not protect himself from the wound of love. Instead, in becoming a man of sorrows, he embraced it. Our very salvation rests on the fact that he was willing to be broken, and heartbroken, for our sake. This is a fact of history, but it is also an ongoing dynamic of our relationship with him. He offers himself not only once for all but also all the time. As E. Lily Yu put it, "Even now He risks our refusal in every moment."[10] He makes himself a perpetual gift that we can receive or reject. For every instance that I respond to his overtures, there are a hundred that I ignore. When I devolve into angry rumination, snap at my children, or wallow in self-pity, I suppress God's kindness toward me and through me to others. I close myself to his love because it feels unsafe or inconvenient or unimpressive.

But still, he waits for me. Still, he offers himself. Undeterred by rejection, Jesus pursues us with dogged determination. By worldly standards we might call this kind of persistence foolish. By theological standards we call it grace.

At the Lord's Table, that grace is made tangible as we hold Jesus' broken body in our hands. We remember his willingness to give himself to the ones who would turn away. We find ourselves in that story as we reflect on the many ways we denied him just last week.

We might even wonder if his grace will be wasted on us, if his love will be ineffectual in the face of our addictions, our unforgiveness, our haunted memories. To our disappointment, this might seem to be the case: we remain stuck in these things unto death. But his gift is proof that somehow, his love has already gone unto death—and risen again. So we receive him, accepting that some questions will remain unanswered for now.

And as we receive him, we find strength to persevere in our own self-giving, despite the unanswered questions this also brings. In choosing to love, will I lose again? If so, who and when and how? Will it be another brother, a child, a friend? Will I get it wrong in my attempts to love, or get it right but be unheard, or both? Lewis concludes,

> There is no safe investment. To love at all is to be vulnerable. Love anything, and your heart will certainly be wrung and possibly be broken. . . . We shall draw nearer to God, not by trying to avoid the sufferings inherent in all loves, but by accepting them and offering them to Him; throwing away all defensive armour. If our hearts need to be broken, and if He chooses this as the way in which they should break, so be it.[11]

I don't know whether our hearts need to be broken, but I know that Jesus' was. I fear becoming like him, but I am compelled to follow, to learn. I am captivated by his courage and his willingness to lose, again and again, for love. In receiving his loss, I find the strength to lose as well.

10

HOME

The Longest Table in the World

---

*For all its rooted loveliness, the world has no continuing
city here; it is an outlandish place, a foreign home, a session
in via to a better version of itself—and it is our glory to
see it so and thirst until Jerusalem comes home at last.*

ROBERT FARRAR CAPON, *THE SUPPER OF THE LAMB*

FOR MOST OF MY CHILDHOOD, I imagined that I would grow up
and move away from my family. In elementary school, this perception was born of wanderlust: I didn't want to leave home as
much as I wanted to travel the world (a desire that partially fueled
my perceived missionary calling). In middle school, when I became
more aware of career choices, I found it odd that some people pre-
ferred staying in their hometown to the possibility of finding more
exciting work elsewhere. Nobody in my large extended family lived
in the same city. My aunts and uncles and grandparents—and
chiefly my father—had all followed jobs around the country.

At least, this was my perception.

As an adult I now realize that some of those aunts and uncles had married people who chose to stay near *their* hometown, and that they probably valued the distance from their own family of origin that this afforded. Sometimes choosing a place to live is more about what we hope to lose than what we hope to find.

My dad's habitual relocations, I think, were motivated by a combination of things. For one, he had his own wanderlust. Nothing was more exciting to him than the horizon. His career led our family from Memphis to Manhattan to St. Louis to Atlanta to Charleston, all by the time I was ten. A perpetual dreamer, he sometimes even floated the idea of Australia to my mother. (I don't know whether he was serious or simply teasing her with this recurring suggestion, but she held her ground regardless.) I struggled with these childhood moves, but I was also drawn in by my father's optimism. His joy in describing the world to me left its mark. He'd imparted his love for horizons; I was ready to move to Australia.

But my father's dreaming also had something of a restless quality to it. His own childhood had its share of trauma, most of which I didn't learn about until after he got sick. In chasing a career and a horizon and a home, I think he was searching for something that had been interrupted for him as a child. He was on a mission to find and re-create for us what he felt he had lacked. I know this, because he used to tell us. This was how he framed our move to coastal South Carolina when I was ten. We weren't just relocating again, we were going *home*. We would build a beautiful house among the oak trees and the marsh and stay there forever.

This plan had a ring of permanence.

Less than a year later, after we moved but before we'd built our house, this plan was interrupted when my dad was diagnosed with cancer.

Though we didn't stay near the coast, we did stay in South Carolina. We moved again to a city further north with more community infrastructure—a location my parents chose in preparation for single parenthood. This is the city where my dad bought the big house that he would eventually die in. It wasn't the setting he initially envisioned, but our last home together was a kind of swan song that still enchanted us all for a season.

For my dad, the idea of home was haunted but also hallowed: He had been running from it, but simultaneously looking for it. For me, home was more elusive. It was an almost-reality that tugged at my heart but never fully delivered on its promises. Just when I began to love a place, we'd move again.

People searching for home is one of the major storylines of the Bible.

In Genesis, God creates humans in a garden called Eden and hands them the keys. They live and work there in the company of God, who "walks" among them in the cool of the day.[1] When they sabotage their relationship with God, the result is exile—from the garden and from God's presence. Now homeless and hungry for the divine connection they previously knew, they attempt to build a new home that will touch heaven by a different route. Eden was a place of intimacy between God and humans, and Babel would be its counterfeit: a human initiative to reach God on their own terms.

In his mercy, God disrupts this project and disperses the people. And he calls one man from among them to leave the only home he has ever known and go to a place that God would show him. Abraham, often called "the father of Israel," becomes a pilgrim in search of a promised land that God is preparing for a new family.

Abraham's sojourn lasts for generations. After his descendants temporarily shelter in Egypt during a famine, they fall into slavery for four hundred years. When God brings them out, their persistent mistrust delays their entrance into the Promised Land for another generation. They wander the desert for forty years, living in tents and worshiping God in a mobile temple. After they finally settle in the land of promise, they again fail to be faithful to the God who brought them there. Again they forfeit their intimacy with him and are sent into exile—this time as captives of a conquering nation.

Seventy years later, God paves the way for them to return to the land, but now it is occupied by a foreign ruler. The Israelites are home, but not in the way they hoped. The Old Testament closes with the Israelites living like exiles in their own country.

Not every reader of Scripture shares Israel's ethnic history. But the Bible's claim is that through Israel, God tells us the story of humanity. We can all trace our lineage to that first human family and its profound loss. We all live in a world that was designed for peace but is currently occupied by a foreign and oppressive power. In the modern West, we may chafe at the idea of exile or of being unable to make and maintain a place of our own. Many of us have been raised with the exact opposite message—as children of the American dream, we've been taught more about the promises of Babel than the echoes of Eden.

But however successful we might seem in our quest to establish ourselves, whatever houses we build or lands we acquire or families we make, we remain haunted by a periodic restlessness—a nagging thought that something is missing or might be taken from us at any moment. It can cause us to move from place to place, searching, as my father once did, or perhaps to lie awake at night worrying about whether our children are still breathing in their beds. In myriad ways, we sense that the home we long for remains just beyond our ability to grasp or protect. As J. R. R. Tolkien wrote in a letter to his son, "Our whole nature at its best and least corrupted, its gentlest and most humane, is still soaked with the sense of 'exile.'"[2]

When I was growing up, I would have attributed my personal sense of exile to the losses I experienced as a child. My family's efforts to settle in "the land" as we imagined it were frustrated by my father's illness, followed by our inability to make house payments after his death.

By the time I was in high school, my childhood notions of moving away had become a full-blown commitment. At a graduation ceremony I attended my freshman year, I noted how many of my elder classmates planned to attend state schools close by. As I watched them receive their diplomas, I vowed to myself that when my graduation came, I would have plans to attend college further away than any of my classmates.

I kept this vow.

I decided on a college in New Jersey. To some of my friends, this seemed about as crazy as my dad wanting to move to Australia. A few specifically feared that I would end up marrying a Yankee, which I did. Because I didn't marry into a Southern family, and because my memories of growing up in the South were all laced with loss, I thought I would never live there again.

In fifteen years of ministry, I have heard a lot of origin stories.

For most people, growing up was a mixed bag of happiness and dysfunction. There are good memories, like the smell of cinnamon rolls baking on Christmas morning, the summer evenings chasing fireflies with siblings, the sweet warble of a grandmother's voice singing in church. But there are also difficult memories. These are harder to articulate but also harder to forget: the silent treatment of a moody parent, the predictable smell of alcohol on adult breath, the loneliness of feeling unseen in a full room.

Given these complex histories, our ambivalence about home makes sense. As a college student in New Jersey, I invited friends to join me on monthly pilgrimages to the closest Chick-fil-A—a forty-five-minute drive—to buy gallons of sweet tea for my dorm room fridge. I felt somehow alienated from my home in the South, but I still wanted a taste of it with me to share with others.

I was fortunate to grow up with innumerable stories to savor and hold near, even while I processed the pain in some of them. But for many people I've met, the scales tip in the other direction. For them, home was not a nest from which to fly; it was a prison from which to escape. They want no taste of it in their mouths. These brave men and women know homesickness of a different kind—they miss the very things they never experienced. Our universal longing for safety, welcome, and belonging are like breadcrumbs that lead us, if not back to our childhood tables, in search of another table altogether. Our hunger for what we've not yet tasted can convince us we're crazy, or it can convince us that food exists.

In my spiritual journey, this other Table dared me to believe that my own experience of home was more than a passing memory. In Christ, I found a belonging that can't be interrupted by cancer or a move to a new city or a poor behavioral record. His love is stronger than death. This love healed my ambivalence by integrating those things I most cherished about my childhood with my ongoing hunger to experience them: I didn't need to hoard the memory of wholeness, because it remained on offer, my daily bread.

The almost-promise that tugged on my heart as a child was a signpost of a more solid reality, a more permanent presence than I knew to hope for growing up. This is true for all of us: The home we knew, as Frederick Buechner coined it, is only a window into the home we dream.[3] One of the great surprises of the gospel is that in his mercy, God continues dreaming for us when the window goes dark.

Under four hundred years of foreign occupation in their own land, the Jews grew weary. Then the Messiah came. But when he finally arrived, his rescue was not what they expected.

Instead of defeating Rome, he died for Rome. Instead of reversing Israel's exile, he entered into it. Jesus left his place of safety and privilege and became homeless for our sake, so that by his faithful life and death he might restore the land—not only to Israel but to the whole human family. Whitney Woollard summarizes:

> On the cross, Jesus fully identifies with our experience of exile and then suffers in our place, dying and rising from the dead to inherit the world and bring humanity back into the promised land. Now those who identify with Jesus through faith and repentance are brought into the presence of God once again and given the world as our inheritance—led by Jesus, the new Adam, into the new Eden.[4]

This rescue was more expansive than God's people remembered to hope for. From the beginning, their true home was not in a particular place as much as it was in a particular presence. Jesus came to restore humanity's communion with God.

But then, Jesus ascended.

On his last night with his disciples, Jesus had promised, "I will not drink again of this fruit of the vine until that day when I drink it new with you in my Father's kingdom."[5] Permanent rest for God's people, then, was deferred until Christ's return. At their earliest eucharistic celebrations, Christians prayed *Maranatha*—"Come, Lord Jesus!"[6]—because they understood this world would not be fully released from captivity until its King returned to finish what he started. From the beginning, the Lord's Supper was soaked with longing for the day that Jesus' friends could sit at table with him again.

For now, they were to continue as sojourners.

For thirteen years, I healed away from home, living happily in a long-distance relationship with my family. After college, my husband Michael and I moved to Texas for four years of seminary, then to a Virginia suburb of Washington, DC, to serve our first church. We hoped, potentially, to settle there.

But then, my brother Noah died. It seemed an incredible gift that he had come to stay with us for a summer and that we happened to live close to where he died so we could host my family's visit to identify his body. But after my mom and siblings got back in their cars to go home, I felt an overwhelming urge not to be far away anymore. Having children had awakened my desire to be closer to my family, and losing my brother made that desire feel more important. Suddenly, what mattered most were these people who I loved and who might not be here a year from now. The only guarantee time gives us is that it is running out; I wanted to be present for whatever time we had left.

Seven months after Noah died, my husband and I prayerfully discerned a move to South Carolina. I laughed through tears at the unmaking of my vow to never return there, and I thanked God for knowing better than me. After many years of chasing the horizon, I was coming *home*.

Leaving Virginia was not easy. I cried for two months as we packed up our house and said our goodbyes. We'd been there for almost five years, and the church where we worked had become like family. Our two sons were born there. We had buried some of Noah's ashes in a memorial garden right outside the sanctuary where we worshiped weekly. Moving further south meant being further from Michael's family in New Jersey. For these reasons, coupled with my newfound commitment to be proximate to my remaining family members, I recognized a new vow forming in my heart: This would be our last move. We were coming home to stay; I was tired of saying goodbye.

In his book *Longing for Home*, Frederick Buechner recounts an odd detail from one of his novels, in which the main character, Antonio, returns home after a season of travel. His young son and some other children have made a sign for him that reads "WELCOME HONE." A loving message, with a slight misspelling. "It seemed oddly fitting," Antonio reflects. "It was good to get home, but it was home with something missing or out of whack about it. It wasn't much, to be sure, just some minor stroke or serif, but even a minor stroke can make a major difference."[7]

Buechner admits that this detail in the story came to him without foresight or planning:

> As I sketched out in my mind that scene in my novel, I thought of it primarily as a scene that would show Antonio Parr's great joy at returning to his home after such a long absence. But then out of nowhere . . . there came into my mind that sign with the missing leg of the *m*. From as deep a place within me as my books and my dreams come from, there came . . . this revelation that although Antonio was enormously glad to be home at last . . . he was in some sense a stranger and an exile there. It is when he comes home that he recognizes most poignantly that he is, at a deep level of his being, homeless, and that whatever it is that is missing, he will spend the rest of his days . . . seeking to find it.[8]

When I moved back to South Carolina, I thought it would be a poignant resolution to a painful childhood. I felt healed and ready to commit to a people and a place and to stay there forever. It was a plan with a ring of permanence, the happy ending I desperately wanted.

But it was not to be.

Three years after we got settled in, the plans and the vows that we made began crumbling in our hands. A pandemic happened. Jobs fell apart. These and other circumstances beyond our control forced us into another season of prayerful discernment. Over time, God made it clear that he was calling us somewhere else.

At first I resisted this call, refusing to recognize that the sign had always read, "WELCOME HONE." The thought of leaving my family again, after finally finding the courage to admit how badly I wanted to be close to them, bewildered me. But for reasons we could not understand, Michael and I both knew that this is what God was asking of us.

In his kindness to me, the Lord called us only one state away, to serve a wonderful church in the mountains of North Carolina. This is the place I am now learning to call home.

But in finding, and losing, a sense of place again and again, I am beginning to realize that wherever I live out the rest of my days will only ever be "hone." There is no place on earth anymore that can seat my entire family around a table, or even protect me from losing more of them. There is no job that can guarantee an untroubled future for my children.

Whether we sojourn or settle, we can't outrun or stave off loss. We can't stop time.

Under the oppressive rule of death, time eventually will take everything: Our houses will sit empty or be torn down altogether. Our loved ones will turn to ash in the ground. We may remember the faces around that once-full table, but even our memories are fading away, despite how we might try to preserve them.

In the book of Hebrews, we read about others who faced similar losses. Abel lost his life to a jealous brother; Noah watched his home wash away in a flood; Abraham obeyed the call to live as a nomad with no knowledge of when it would end. These men "died in faith . . . having acknowledged that they were strangers and exiles on the earth."

But in their witness, we find more than loss:

> For people who speak thus make it clear that they are seeking a homeland. If they had been thinking of that land from which they had gone out, they would have had opportunity to return. But as it is, they desire a better country . . . a heavenly one. Therefore God is not ashamed to be called their God, for he has prepared for them a city. (Heb 11:13-16)

God has always promised a place for his people—but even now, we are still waiting to take hold of it. We are still waiting for him to renew time and space with his healing touch. Our true resting place can't be found by chasing the horizon or by cherishing the past; it can only be found in the One who holds these things together. *He* is the only home we really have. One day he will return to us, bringing our memories and dreams with him. In his presence, everything we've lost will be healed and whole and alive. And everything we never had to begin with but knew we needed—a better country—will be ours to inhabit without fear. We won't be exiles there. He is preparing for us a city. When we see it, the sign will finally read: "WELCOME HOME." On that day, there won't be any more goodbyes.

For now, the Christian life is like living out of a suitcase.

We are called to be fully present where we are, to "seek the welfare" of our neighborhoods and cities.[9] And yet we know that we aren't sovereign over these places or the people within them—that they, too, are captives of an age that is subject to decay. We are invited to settle in, but without fully unpacking our belongings. The land is ours, but the house is still being built.

This is hard work.

In many ways, it is the original human challenge: to whole-heartedly love the world God gave us without making it an idol. When our first parents decided they needed the fruit of the tree more than they needed the closeness of God, they failed to rightly order their priorities. When we elevate any of God's gifts—blessings like a spouse, a child, a hometown, a career—to a place of primacy in our lives, we are seeking a city without foundations.

These things can never bear the weight of our well-being.

In reaction to this, sometimes we err in the other direction. We practice such a thorough detachment from the material world that we fall short of loving the very things God has called us to love. We refuse to open our hearts to the beauty around us, believing instead that we must save ourselves for a far-off "heavenly home."

In her book *This Homeward Ache*, Amy Baik Lee describes the learned temporariness of frequent moves and her reticence to fully enjoy the first house they bought for their family: "I am surprised to discover how hesitant I am to let myself love this place. I tell myself I want to hold it loosely, knowing that the Lord I follow had 'nowhere to lay his head.' . . . But if I'm honest, my stance is also a defense; a loose grasp will make things easier if a catastrophe strikes or we have to move on someday."[10] It was the writing of Anthony Esolen that helped her embrace the tension inherent in the call. She quotes him: "We have no abiding place on earth. But that does not mean that we are to love no place at all."[11]

How do we keep our hearts alive to what we know we will lose? How do exiles learn the art of homemaking?

When the Israelites were sojourning from Egypt, they knew they were headed toward a fertile and free homeland. God had told them it was a "good and broad" place, "flowing with milk and honey."[12] But the journey was hard and the desert was hot. Along the way, they wondered if captivity in Egypt was actually preferable to hunger and homelessness on the road. In response, God provided manna for them to eat.

We've already seen how this miracle bread met their physical needs and bolstered their faith in God's provision. But biblical scholars note another detail about the manna and therefore its meaning for God's people: It tasted "like wafers made with honey."[13] Brant Pitre elaborates, "Why did the manna taste like honey? The answer is simple, but important: it was a foretaste of the promised land—the 'land flowing with milk and honey.' In other words, by means of the manna, God was calling the Israelites to place their trust in his ability . . . to see them home."[14]

In our long sojourn, we also have been given a heavenly meal.

The Lord's Supper doesn't fully ease the discomfort of this in-between place in which we live, but it does nourish us with the life of the One who became homeless for our sake. Jesus knows the ache of exile, homelessness, and loss. He embraced these things so that we could ultimately be rescued from them. When we take the bread that Jesus called the true manna, we receive the strength to follow him to the land that he has prepared for us.[15] The Eucharist reminds us that God's provision here and now isn't a finish line; it's the sustenance to keep putting one foot in front of the other on the trail that he has blazed.

But that sustenance is more than mere utility. It also comforts us with a taste of our ultimate home. Our celebrations around the Lord's Table whet our appetite for the final feast that Jesus is preparing upon his return. "The Lord's Supper," writes J. Todd Billings, "as a foretaste of the wedding banquet of the lamb and his bride, gives us a taste of God's New World."[16] This taste is both familiar to us and foreign: The ordinariness of bread and wine is evidence that whatever God's new world will be, it will bear some resemblance to this one. Like the sweet tea that comforted me in college, there will be aspects of the home we knew in the home we dream. The things we've loved along the way, insofar as they belong to him, won't be lost but transfigured in the age to come. This emboldens us to open our hearts to the world we know now, because we understand even if we can't hold onto it, he can and will.

But new creation also contains flavors that our palates can't yet name. We don't yet know what eternity tastes like. We've not yet lived in a place where "death shall be no more," where crying and mourning and pain have passed away, where all things are made new. This is how Revelation describes the city that is coming, the "new Jerusalem" where God will dwell with us forever.[17]

This future is not just a plan, it's a promise. I don't pretend to understand it. But in our shared Supper, I do believe that we are glimpsing it, even if only in part.

In Celtic spirituality, there's an ancient recognition of "thin places," where the veil between heaven and earth is especially translucent. Thin places are believed to create a particularly hospitable environment for sensing God's presence. The Lord's Table is such a place. We find it in grand sanctuaries with stained glass windows and in borrowed school cafeterias where new congregations gather. We find it in beautiful mountain towns and in war-torn countries; in national cathedrals and in illegal underground churches. In every place that God's people gather to commune with him, heaven touches earth and we experience, in part, the fellowship that characterizes our forever home.

A colleague of mine used to say that the Eucharist creates "the longest table in the world." It was his way of reminding us that there are people communing with Jesus on another side of the Table, just beyond the veil. We can't see them now, but one day we will. My father is among them and also, I believe, my brother, my grandmother, and countless children of God I've yet to meet. Some days this veil feels especially thin to me, and I can sense their presence. Most days it doesn't. But when I take the bread and the wine, I am reminded that the full table I long for is real and is coming. And that is enough for now.

LET US KEEP
THE FEAST

WHEN I WAS WRITING THIS BOOK, I met a friendly older gentleman at the local library where I did a lot of my work. He asked me a barrage of questions about my profession and my project, then finally conceded, "I'm a lifelong churchgoer, but I've never understood the point of the Lord's Supper." I appreciated his honesty, and I imagine plenty of Christians can relate to his secret confusion.

After a few minutes of conversation about it, we agreed that whether or not we understand the point of the Supper, we continue to celebrate it because Jesus told us to do so. My kids don't see the point of brushing their teeth (despite my frequent attempts to compel—or threaten—them toward oral health), but they do it out of obedience. Often, Christianity is this simple. We walk by faith, not by sight.

When I began receiving weekly Communion, I didn't have much to say about it yet. I was merely participating in the rhythms of my new church. Over time, it was the *experience* that informed my understanding—as I came forward to receive, as I watched my brothers and sisters kneel beside me at the rail, I became aware that something was happening that I didn't fully understand. I was being conscripted into a story that I couldn't yet articulate with words, but that I knew was somehow changing me.

It is good to think deeply about the meaning of our faith and its accompanying practices. But often, meaning can't be truly understood apart from experience. To apprehend something, we must enter into it. We don't really know how to ride a bike until we feel it in our bodies. The invitation of the gospel is the same: When Jesus was questioned by John's disciples, he didn't explain everything up front. He said, "Come and you will see."[1] At the Lord's Table, we respond to that invitation in one small way. We move toward an encounter, whether or not we understand exactly what it means, how it will (or won't) feel, or what difference it might make. We enter into the mystery on offer.

As a pastor, I do believe that the Eucharist uniquely helps us to understand and experience the gospel. In my own life, taking Communion allowed me to receive God's love not only in my mind but in my body—and in the body of believers around me. In remembering Christ the way he instructed, we are *re-membered*, put back together as whole persons and as a people.

But the Eucharist, and the real grace it conveys to us, is still not a "fix all."

Robust observance of the sacraments, as important as they are, will not solve all our problems or magically perfect our faith. In leaving us this meal, Jesus wasn't promising a one-and-done solution for spiritual wholeness. He was providing daily bread.

A friend of mine who is both a priest and a chef loves to point out that when Jesus was born, he was placed in a feeding trough. From his birth, Jesus has been given as food for the world. His self-offering gives us literal and spiritual life—it restores us to God and raises us from the dead, but it also secures a *quality* of life that, even now, in every other form of nourishment, we tend to seek.

"The most splendid dinner, the most exquisite food, the most gratifying company, arouse more appetites than they satisfy," writes

Robert Farrar Capon. This is a kind of hunger, he says, "for which earth has no cure—that major, vaster burning by which the heart looks out astonished at the world and, in its loving, wakes and breaks at once."[2] By taking up residence in this world, Jesus pointed us beyond it. He showed us that our "vast burning" is ordered toward another world altogether. In Christ, we discover that heaven is real and on offer: "I am the living bread that came down from heaven. . . . The bread that I will give for the life of the world is my flesh."[3] His invitation interprets our persistent yearning. It explains why our thirst remains unslaked even after we've drained the dregs of every worldly gift.

Jesus' sole ability to satisfy our hunger is at the heart of the Christian message. And yet, this is a message that we often forget. In big and small ways, we follow our cravings to lesser forms of nourishment. We hope to satiate our search for significance, fulfillment, and belonging in more immediate ways. Or we try to numb our desire for these things through distraction and avoidance. My tendency to turn to my smartphone as soon as I wake up or when I can't sleep at night can be motivated by either of these temptations depending on the day. What am I looking for in this tiny screen? Evidence that I am worthwhile and loved by others? Or an entertaining diversion from the worries I could otherwise name before God?

No matter how long we've been following Jesus, we still need practice recognizing and reordering our appetites. We need to be reminded that there is another, better provision than the ones we've tasted for so long.

At the Lord's Supper, we rehearse the truth about ourselves and our God. He alone can satisfy the world's deep ache. He is the Bread of Life. This might be one reason Jesus gave us a practice to repeat: We don't get baptized every week, but we do come to the Table again and again—because the repetition helps to retrain our palates.

It teaches us, over time, to get in touch with our deep hunger and to recognize that nothing else can fill it.

When I first began receiving Communion regularly, I was noticing different hungers than I am today. At twenty-three, I was navigating the impact of childhood losses that now are largely healed. At thirty-six, I am growing as a mom, a priest, a writer, a wife, and a member of a new community. On any given Sunday, one or more of these areas of my life has likely exposed my great deficiency and my great need for God's mercy. I can suppress my awareness of this, insisting that I have no insecurities or frustrations. Or I can open my hands and ask Jesus to fill my great lack. My children cannot fill me. My ministry cannot fill me.

Only Jesus can make us whole.

I know that he will never withhold himself from me, or from any who come to him in faith. And yet, I also know that the bread in my hands is only a foretaste of the fullness to come. Our salvation is here, our satisfaction in Jesus is available now, and yet the shadow of sin and death still lingers. Our faith will continue to falter. Our bodies will continue to decay. This is true because the Table conscripts us into a story that isn't over yet: Jesus has given himself fully, but we have yet to see him face to face.

Today's eucharistic celebrations (and spiritual disciplines, and Christian community) can't satiate us completely; rather, they sustain us until he comes. So we keep showing up—not because we think that if we just show up long enough or in exactly the right way then the struggle will end—but because we know that in the struggle, there is One who will continue to meet us and strengthen us *until* the end.

When I buried my brother's ashes in the memorial garden at my church in Virginia, I was accompanied only by my husband and a dear pastor and his wife. We held our own quiet ceremony for him on the Feast of the Holy Innocents, a somber day just after Christmas that remembers the children King Herod murdered in his bloodlust for the infant Jesus. We huddled in the cold while my husband dug a shallow grave in the frozen dirt. Then we drove home. There was no music or procession. There was no gravestone or marker to designate where we laid him. I wondered if I might forget the exact spot over the years.

Later that spring, just before Holy Week, our church installed outdoor Stations of the Cross around campus—beautiful images depicting different scenes from Jesus' last day on earth. For centuries, Christians have used Stations of the Cross as a sort of contemplative prayer walk; we slowly move from one station to the next, following Jesus in our imaginations as he journeys toward his death. The fourteenth and final station, "Jesus Is Laid in the Tomb," was erected in the memorial garden. Directly in front of where my brother was buried now stands a picture of Jesus' lifeless face, waiting for resurrection.

As strange as it may sound, this sad image comforts me. It reminds me that because Jesus was willing to die as one of us, our own deaths can be infused with hope—their permanence reframed as a pregnant pause.

Of course, Jesus resting in the grave isn't the most *precise* picture of Christian hope: Our faith is built on the belief that Jesus no longer waits in the tomb. But others of us, like my brother, still do. And all of us, whether we live or die, are waiting in one way or another. We are waiting for healed relationships, freedom from temptation, societal renewal, restored bodies. All of us are waiting for our faith to be made sight. We are waiting for the end of the story. In his resurrection, Jesus has promised us exactly what that end will look like. And in the meal he has given to sustain us in the meantime, he has shown us exactly how to wait.

One of Jesus' few postresurrection conversations hints at this.

After appearing to his disciples and joining them for breakfast on the beach, while they are still wild with joy, Jesus speaks to Peter about the work to which Jesus is now calling him. He asks, "Simon, son of John, do you love me?" Peter responds, "Yes, Lord; you know that I love you."

Jesus says, "Feed my lambs."[4]

Peter and his friends might have thought Jesus' resurrection was the grand finale of the story—and in some ways it was—but for the church, the work was about to begin in earnest. Jesus had conquered death, but that wouldn't prevent his people from experiencing it themselves as they followed him. Peter himself would be martyred not long after this poignant conversation. Jesus knew that as we learn to follow our Shepherd, we need to be nourished with his life.

We need to be fed.

This nourishment—of word and sacrament, of Jesus' presence by his Spirit and through his people—sustains us, like it sustained those first disciples who feasted with Jesus on the beach in the joy of his resurrection. The memory of his newly beating heart warmed them, and it whispered the promise of his return, as they went on to carry their own crosses. Each Eucharist, then, is a taste of that Easter joy—however distant it may seem in our current experience—and a fulfillment of Jesus' final request: "Feed my lambs."

Our Shepherd knows the challenges we face as we await him. He knows that we are embattled and that some of us are in graves. As we break the bread that foretells our final healing, we don't expect the ache of the present age to vanish completely. But we do learn to carry our crosses with hope. Our griefs, our unresolved questions, our unmet longings will one day be caught up and recast in the great light of the age to come. When we see him, our graves will be empty and our hearts will be whole.

Until then, let us keep the feast.

ACKNOWLEDGMENTS

THIS BOOK REFLECTS MANY YEARS of life and many people who nurtured my faith during a vulnerable season. I want to begin by thanking the men and women who were present to my family and me during and after my dad's illness: you know who you are, but you will never know the extent of your ministry to us. To my aunts and uncles, grandparents, and friends who "adopted" me into your homes and lives, thank you. And thank you to my high school teachers and mentors who patiently knocked sense into me and helped me find strength. I couldn't write this book without thinking of you and the impact you've had on my life.

Thank you to InterVarsity Press for the opportunity to share this story with a larger audience and to my editor, Ted Olsen, for being an early and enduring believer in it. Thank you also to Ethan McCarthy for first inviting me to put this idea on paper. Esau McCaulley, thank you for inspiring me through your many writings and for encouraging me by writing this book's foreword.

Special thanks to my father-in-law, Gordon King, for funding my research library full of niche and out of-print books. I could never have written all those footnotes without you.

Thank you to my writing friends, especially Courtney Ellis for being a tireless encourager and question-answerer, Chrystie Cole for reading every word of the manuscript in real time, and Lindsey Jones for lending wisdom and humor in expert combination. To the friends who read chapters or early drafts in advance, thank you for the time and care you invested in my words. To the many other friends who told me for years, "you should write a book one day," thank you for seeing this before I could.

To my prayer team, for reading so many emails and for remembering me so often before the Father: You helped me write this book in the most supernatural way! Jim and Nadine Maxwell, thank you for being such enduring cheerleaders. Beth Bryant, my "book therapist," thank you for helping me navigate the complexities of sharing a deeply personal story with the world.

To the congregations I have served and whose stories are represented in this book: All Saints, Truro, and Village Anglican churches, thank you for allowing me to share life with you and to learn from you. I am especially grateful to The Vine Anglican Church, for giving me a soft landing in North Carolina to write this book and for welcoming my family so well into your community. Thank you also for calling us to such a beautiful part of the world.

To the friends and teachers whose ideas have shaped my own, including Bob Good, Esther Meek and the professors at Redeemer Seminary, Aaron Williams, Pauline Buisch, and Sue Hardman: Thank you for sharing your beautiful minds with me. A special thank you also to Carol Davis for your faithful discipleship through these many years and to Rhiannon Poore for your friendship and encouragement in many forms before, during, and after the writing process.

To my siblings, thank you for being the only people in the world who share this story with me in the unique way that we do. Dad was right—you turned out to be my best friends. And to my mom, the invisible character in most of these chapters: Thank you for being there. Thank you for still being here, and for answering my phone calls even when you're making a smoothie.

Thank you to my children, Isaiah, David, and Esther, for being excited with me and for praying the same prayer every night for a year ("Please help Mom's book be good"). You are my best teachers; I hope this book teaches you a little bit about the love from which you come and for which you were born.

And to my husband, Michael: You are God's best gift to me. Thank you for your profound generosity and enduring support, especially in the writing of this book. You know I'm crying.

Lastly, thanks be to God, for being the chief author of this story. Thank you for allowing us to share your Table as sons and daughters. Give us grace to always remain there.

QUESTIONS FOR REFLECTION AND DISCUSSION

THESE QUESTIONS CAN BE USED as journal prompts or for discussion with others. Choose the ones that resonate with you.

1. HOPE

1. What "scripts" or formulas are you aware of that shape your expectations for your life or the expectations of people in your culture generally?

2. What crises or experiences have challenged your personal or faith paradigm? What new "scripts" have they given you, if any?

3. In your experience of Christian hope, have you tended more toward an expectation for renewal or patience in suffering? Can you think of a person or a season in which you saw these things held in tension?

4. The author suggests that for the first Christians, the Lord's Supper was "equal parts remembrance and longing." In what ways specifically might the Supper stir your longing for Jesus' return?

5. The author closes the chapter by saying, "a life yielded to God is a eucharistic life." What do you think of this idea? What might it look like in your story?

2. ENCOUNTER

1. Who are some of the people whose "gaze" helped to form you, for good or for ill?

2. In what ways has your life or your faith been shaped by consumerism?

3. Are there specific blessings you have felt God owes you or that you expected to receive from him in response to your obedience? What would it look like to name your feelings about that to him?

4. To what extent do you want God, not just his "stuff"—his blessings? And to what extent do you believe that he wants you, apart from your accomplishments?

5. When you imagine your relationship with God, are there things you tend to hide behind to feel more worthy, to prevent rejection, or to justify yourself?

6. Dr. Curt Thompson said, "We are born into the world looking for someone who is looking for us." How has this been true in your life?

7. Have you ever experienced or understood Communion as an intimate encounter with Jesus? Why or why not?

3. EMBODIMENT

1. What did you grow up believing about God's plan for our bodies and/or the material world?

2. What ways have you experienced the denigration of material creation or of your own body? How have you participated in that denigration, either consciously or subconsciously?

3. How might the incarnation change the way you think about embodiment?

4. What story does your body have to tell? How do you think Jesus would respond to that story or perhaps change it?

5. Olivier Clement called Communion "resurrection food." How might the Lord's Supper inform your expectations regarding bodily renewal, either now or when Jesus returns?

4. GIFT

1. How would you describe your relationship with joy?

2. The author describes joy as "prophetic." Think of a time when you experienced or witnessed a kind of joy that authentically transcended present circumstances. What did this look like (and what did it not look like)?

3. The author says, "God is not a taskmaster—he is a banquet-master." How does this claim resonate with or challenge you?

4. In what ways or areas do you want to get better at lament? At celebration? How can the church more broadly improve in these disciplines as well?

5. Look online for a picture of *The Disciples Peter and John Running to the Sepulchre on the Morning of the Resurrection* by Eugène Bernand. Spend some time contemplating it.

5. COMMUNITY, PART 1

1. When you think of family, what experiences or feelings (positive or negative) come to the surface?

2. How have you seen the church function—or fail to function—as a family?

3. The author suggests that nuclear families are important but that if they aren't subordinated within the broader family of faith, they can become an idol. What are the biggest challenges Christians face in getting this balance right?

4. If Communion isn't just about an individual's relationship with God, but about God's relationship with a community, how can Communion help us grow in relationship with each other?

5. Who in the household of faith has "familied" you? To whom might God be calling you to turn toward as a mother, father, sister, or brother?

6. Community, Part 2

1. When or how have you felt disillusioned by the church? What led to that feeling?

2. Why do you think Jesus is willing to stick with his people even when they hurt his reputation?

3. Mike Cosper wrote that it's "easier to cherry pick reality than watch a dream die." In what ways might this be relevant to your relationship with church? Are there any dreams you need to let die?

4. Communion is the fellowship of a reconciled people: to each other and to God. Is there anyone in the fellowship of faith you need to reconcile with? What steps can you take to do that? If it's not possible to take those steps now, how is God leading you to pray about this broken relationship?

5. Read 1 Corinthians 11:17-34. How does this change the way you approach the Communion table? How does it impact the way you see your pastor?

6. What does it mean to say the creedal words "I believe in the church"?

7. Abundance

1. How has fear of scarcity impacted your life? How do you see it impacting our culture?

2. The Hebrews hoarded manna in the desert because they didn't trust God to provide it again the next day. In what areas or ways are you still learning to trust God's promises?

3. When Mary was pregnant with Jesus, she prayed, "God has filled the hungry with good things, and the rich he has sent away empty" (Lk 1:53). How is this true in a world where people are still starving?

4. Jesus' feeding of the five thousand echoes back to the hungry Hebrews in the wilderness and forward to the Last Supper. How do these echoes change the way you read the stories? How do they change the way you understand the Lord's Supper?

5. Is there an area or situation in which Jesus is calling you to offer up your meager resources for his distribution? What would obedience to that call look like?

8. Hospitality

1. Has God ever called you to something before you felt ready?

2. The author says, "the Christian life is about more than recovery. We are called to ministry." How does this claim resonate with or challenge you?

3. How has God shown hospitality to you? How has the gospel taken shape specifically in your life? How has God uniquely equipped or called you to show gospel hospitality to others?

4. How might the Eucharist enrich the way we understand Christian mission?

5. Think of a situation when you started out as the giver/host but ended up being the guest/receiver.

6. The author says, "the ultimate act of hospitality is to allow ourselves to become, in God's hands, bread for breaking." Who in your life has become this "broken bread" for you? Whom is God now nourishing through you?

7. Look up Andrei Rublev's icon *The Trinity* and spend some time contemplating it.

9. Courage

1. When has your love for someone else taken a different shape than you expected it to?

2. The author describes the "'happily-ever-after' thinking" that sometimes characterizes the evangelical imagination. Have you experienced this? Have you been let down by it?

3. Jesus' life didn't end in validation or resolution, but in rejection and betrayal. How might this part of the gospel story challenge us? How might it comfort us?

4. What would it look like for you specifically to focus more on obedience than outcomes in the Christian life?

5. Think about Jesus' perpetual self-offering to his people, knowing that we often reject him in big and small ways. Think also about his ultimate vindication and confidence that he will "lose nothing" of what the Father has given him (Jn 6:39). How do we locate ourselves—and our call to love— in that tension?

10. Home

1. What was your experience of home growing up? What do you feel when you think about "home" now?

2. What strikes you the most about the Israelites' layered history of exile and homesickness in the biblical story?

3. In what ways do you observe restlessness in our culture? In what ways do you see people trying to resolve it?

4. What do you expect will be familiar about the new heavens and earth, and what do you think will be different? Consider your own experience as you reflect on this question.

5. Do you tend toward being overly attached to your present experience of earth or overly detached?

6. What about "the longest table in the world" gives you hope?

7. The author describes the Communion table as a "thin place" between heaven and earth. What could this mean for you?

NOTES

PROLOGUE

[1]Anglican Church of Kenya, *Our Modern Services* (Uzima Press, 2002), 83.

[2]See Mt 6:9.

[3]Ps 34:8.

[4]Rom 8:24-25.

[5]1 Cor 13:12.

[6]See Psalm 23:5.

1. HOPE

[1]See Mt 7:7-11.

[2]See Eph 1:11.

[3]See Mt 26:29.

[4]See Acts 2:24.

[5]1 Pet 5:9-10.

[6]Jn 16:33 NIV.

[7]A meaningful foundation for this concept can be found in Geerhardus Vos, *Biblical Theology: Old and New Testaments* (Wipf and Stock, 2003), 381-84.

[8]Esau McCaulley, "I Have Only One Hope for Racial Justice: A God Who Conquered Death," *Christianity Today,* June 10, 2020, www.christianitytoday.com /ct/2020/june-web-only/george-floyd-racial-justice-hope-god-who-conquered -death.html.

[9]C. S. Lewis, *The Weight of Glory: And Other Addresses* (HarperCollins, 1976) chap. 1, Kindle.

[10]See Col 1:17.

[11]For a good introduction to this idea, see Jenn Pollock Michel, *Surprised by Paradox: The Promise of "And" in an Either-Or World* (InterVarsity Press, 2019).

[12]See 1 Cor 11:23-24.

[13]Mt 26:39.

[14]Mt 27:46.

2. ENCOUNTER

[1]Curt Thompson, *The Soul of Shame: Retelling the Stories We Believe About Ourselves* (InterVarsity Press, 2015), 138.

[2]Eve Dupierrix et al., "Preference for Human Eyes in Human Infants," *Journal of Experimental Child Psychology,* vol. 123 (July 2014), www.sciencedirect.com /science/article/pii/S0022096513002737.

[3]John Macmurray, *Persons in Relation* (Humanity Books, 1999), 17, 46-61.

[4]Thompson, *Soul of Shame,* 52, 137.

[5]Saint Augustine, *Confessions,* trans. Henry Chadwick (Oxford University Press, 1991), 3.

[6]James K. A. Smith, *You Are What You Love: The Spiritual Power of Habit* (Brazos, 2016), 46, 50.

[7]See Phil 4:6.

[8]See Rev 21:3.

[9]Rankin Wilbourne discusses the significance of this question in relation to God's quest to unite us to himself in Rankin Wilbourne, *Union with Christ: The Way to Know and Enjoy God* (David C. Cook, 2016), 82.

[10]See Eph 5:31-32.

[11]Sheldon Vanauken, *A Severe Mercy* (Harper and Row, 1977), chap. 2.

[12]Vanauken, *A Severe Mercy,* 210.

[13]Vanauken, *A Severe Mercy,* 219.

[14]Alexander Schmemann, *For the Life of the World: Sacraments and Orthodoxy* (St. Vladimir's Seminary Press, 1963), 14.

[15]Anglican priest and spiritual director Summer Gross has explored the connection between our attachment style and our relationship with God in *The Emmanuel Promise: Discovering the Security of a Life Held by God* (Baker Books, 2024), esp. chap. 1.

[16]Esther Meek, *Loving to Know: Covenant Epistemology* (Cascade, 2011), 306.

[17]See Rom 5:10-11.

[18]I am grateful to Bishop Robert Barron for introducing me to this linguistic analogy in his Easter sermon on John 21. Robert Barron, "Gospel Reflections," Cycle C, 7th week of Easter, June 3, 2022, www.wordonfire.org/reflections/friday -june-3-2022.

[19]See 1 Cor 13:12.

[20]*The Book of Common Prayer* (Anglican Liturgy Press, 2019), 134.

[21]Thomspon, *Soul of Shame,* 138.

3. EMBODIMENT

[1]See Gen 1.

[2]Alexander Schmemann, *For the Life of the World: Sacraments and Orthodoxy* (St. Vladimir's Seminary Press, 1963), 16.

[3]One such philosophy that especially sought to attach to Christianity was Gnosticism. For a fuller treatment of the Gnostic threat and the church's response, see Marcellino D'Ambrosio, *When the Church Was Young: Voices of the Early Fathers* (Servant Books, 2014), chap. 8, Kindle.

[4]N. T. Wright, *Surprised by Hope: Rethinking Heaven, the Resurrection, and the Mission of the Church* (HarperOne, 2008), 199.

[5]Tertullian, *On the Resurrection of the Flesh* 8, cited in Christopher Hall, *Worshiping with the Church Fathers* (InterVarsity Press, 2009), 53.

[6]Hall, *Worshiping with the Church Fathers*, 52-53.

[7]See Col 1:15.

[8]Rom 8:20-21.

[9]Elizabeth Barrett Browning, *Aurora Leigh* (Oxford University Press, 1993), 246.

[10]In the Anglican tradition, children who have been baptized are usually invited to participate in the Lord's Supper at their parents' discretion.

[11]"About Sexual Violence: Quick Facts and Stats," The Centers for Disease Control and Prevention, January 23, 2024, www.cdc.gov/sexual-violence/about/?CDC _AAref_Val=https://www.cdc.gov/violenceprevention/sexualviolence/fastfact.html#.

[12]A good introduction to the science of trauma can be found in Bessel Van Der Kolk, *The Body Keeps the Score* (Penguin Random House, 2014).

[13]2 Cor 5:8.

[14]Lk 23:43.

[15]See Ps 13.

[16]See Phil 4:8.

[17]See Joel 2:25.

[18]Claude Atcho, *Reading Black Books: How African American Literature Can Make Our Faith More Whole and Just* (Brazos Press, 2022), chap. 4, Kindle.

[19]This section and parts of the following are adapted from Hannah King, "Body, Broken: Violence, Trauma and the Eucharist," *The Living Church*, May 25, 2021, https://livingchurch.org/covenant/body-broken/.

[20]Ps 139:7-10 NIV.

[21]Edward Shillito, *Jesus of the Scars: And Other Poems* (Hodder and Stoughton, 1919).

[22]See 1 Cor 15:20.

[23]See Rom 8:23.

[24]Olivier Clement, *The Roots of Christian Mysticism* (New City Press, 1995), 107.

4. Gift

[1]Edward Zwick, dir., *Blood Diamond*, Warner Brothers, 2006.

[2]Michael Lewis, "Don't Eat the Fortune Cookie," Baccalaureate remarks, Princeton University, 2012, www.princeton.edu/news/2012/06/03/princeton-universitys -2012-baccalaureate-remarks.

[3]See Jas 1:17.

[4]Alexander Schmemann, *The Eucharist: Sacrament of the Kingdom* (St. Vladimir's Seminary Press, 1987), 165-69.

[5]Robert Louis Wilken, *The Spirit of Early Christian Thought: Seeking the Face of God* (Yale University Press, 2003), 46.

[6]Tim Keller, "Lord of the Wine," November 17, 1996, https://gospelinlife.com /sermon/lord-of-the-wine/.

[7]C. S. Lewis, *Letters to Malcolm: Chiefly on Prayer* (HarperOne, 2017), chap. 27, Kindle.

[8]George Herbert, "Love (III)," *The Works of George Herbert* (Oxford University Press, 1941), 266.

[9]Tish Harrison Warren, *Prayer in the Night: For Those Who Work or Watch or Weep* (InterVarsity Press, 2021), 151.

[10]In J. R. R. Tolkien's *The Return of the King*, Sam Gamgee falls into a deep sleep after helping Frodo destroy the ring. When he wakes up, he sees a friend he thought was dead: "Gandalf! I thought you were dead! But then I thought I was dead myself. Is everything sad going to come untrue?" J. R. R. Tolkien, *The Return of the King* (Riverside Press, 1965), 230.

[11]*The Disciples Peter and John Running to the Sepulchre on the Morning of the Resurrection* by Eugéne Burnand.

[12]Michael Frost, "Is This the Greatest Easter Painting of All Time?" *Michael Frost* (blog), April 12, 2017, https://mikefrost.net/greatest-easter-painting-time /#comments.

5. Community, Part 1

[1]Mt 12:48-50.

[2]1 Cor 10:16.

[3]See Eph 5:22–6:4; 1 Tim 5:8.

[4]1 Tim 3:1-12.

[5]See 1 Cor 7: 7-40.

[6]For a robust introduction to the ideas in this section, see Emily Hunter McGowin, *Households of Faith: Practicing Family in the Kingdom of God* (InterVarsity Press, 2025), esp. chap. 3.

[7]Ex 4:22; Is 54:5-8.

[8]Is 49:15; 63:16-17.

[9]In his book *The Prayers of Jesus*, German theologian Joachim Jeremias argued that although it was not outside the realm of possibility for a Jewish individual to pray to God as his or her father, Old Testament Judaism overwhelmingly emphasized the relationship between God and the nation. The exception to this was Israel's King, who had a unique, privileged relationship with God. See Joachim Jeremias, *The Prayers of Jesus* (Fortress Press, 1978), 21.

[10]Rom 8:15.

[11]Mk 10:29-30.

[12]Jn 1:13.

[13]Paul Bradshaw and Maxwell Johnson, *The Eucharistic Liturgies: Their Evolution and Interpretation* (Liturgical Press, 2012), 24.

[14]Christine Pohl, *Making Room: Recovering Hospitality as a Christian Tradition* (Eerdmans, 1990), 42.

[15]Gal 3:26, 28-29.

[16]See, for example, Bradshaw and Johnson, *The Eucharistic Liturgies*, 58.

[17]Peter Leithart, *Blessed Are the Hungry: Meditations on the Lord's Supper* (Canon Press, 2000), 157-58.

[18]Gannon Sims, *Bringing Church Home: How the Family of God Makes Us a Little More Human* (Seedbed, 2022), 95.

[19]David Brooks, "The Nuclear Family Was a Mistake," *The Atlantic*, March 2020, www.theatlantic.com/magazine/archive/2020/03/the-nuclear-family-was -a-mistake/605536/.

[20]Brenda B. Colijn, "Family in the Bible: A Brief Survey," *Ashland Theological Journal*, 2004, https://biblicalstudies.org.uk/pdf/ashland_theological_journal /36-1_073.pdf.

6. COMMUNITY, PART 2

[1]Tish Harrison Warren, "True Story," *The Point Magazine*, December 15, 2017, https://thepointmag.com/examined-life/true-story/.

[2]Acts 9:4-5.

[3]See Mt 18:6; Rev 3:13-18.

[4]Mt 24:31.

[5]Dietrich Bonhoeffer, *Life Together: The Classic Exploration of Faith in Community* (Fortress Press, 2015), 13.

[6]Bonhoeffer, *Life Together*, 26-27.

[7]Mike Cosper, *Land of My Sojourn: The Landscape of a Faith Lost and Found* (InterVarsity Press, 2024), 57.

[8]These words come from a liturgy for confession of sin in the Book of Common Prayer.

[9]Alexander Schmemann, *The Eucharist: Sacrament of the Kingdom* (St. Vladimir's Seminary Press, 1987), 139.

[10]Mt 5:23-24.

[11]Fleming Rutledge, *Three Hours: Sermons for Good Friday* (Eerdmans, 2019), third sermon, Kindle.

[12]See 1 Cor 11:17-34.

[13]Laurence Stookey, *Eucharist: Christ's Feast Within the Church* (Abingdon Press, 1993), chap. 1, Kindle.

[14]In Hebrews 12:5-6, we learn that chastisement can be a form of God's love for those he considers sons. This is similar to Paul's promise in 1 Corinthians 11:32 that God's judgment of Christians is ordered toward our discipline and correction.

[15]As Rowan Williams pointed out in *Tokens of Trust: An Introduction to Christian Belief* (Westminster John Knox Press, 2007), 105, the original Greek language of the creeds is better translated, "I *believe* the church"—we can believe its witness about Jesus Christ. But the common English translation is a provocative reminder that the church is God's creation, a work that he will complete on the day of Christ's return.

[16]*Didache* 9:4, trans. Charles H. Hoole, https://pages.uoregon.edu/sshoemak/321 /texts/didache.html.

[17]Catholic and Orthodox Christians do not receive Communion in Protestant parishes, but there are also members of my own denomination who, because of their conviction about women's ordination, do not receive Communion from female priests. I have written more about this in an article titled "I'm a Female Priest and I Support My Opponents in the Women's Ordination Debate," which is now available on my website, www.hannahmillerking.com/blog /im-a-female-priest-and-i-support-my-opponents-in-the-womens-ordination -debate.

7. ABUNDANCE

[1]Danielle Gallegos et al., "Food Insecurity and Child Development: A State-of-the-Art Review," *International Journal of Environmental Research and Public Health*, August 26, 2021, www.ncbi.nlm.nih.gov/pmc/articles/PMC8431639/.

[2]Ex 13:5.

[3]Ex 16:16, 19-20.

[4]Walter Brueggemann, "The Liturgy of Abundance, the Myth of Scarcity," *Christian Century*, March 1999, www.christiancentury.org/article/2012-01/liturgy-abundance-myth-scarcity.

[5]Ex 14:12.

[6]Brueggeman, "Liturgy of Abundance."

[7]Lk 1:53.

[8]Mk 6:35.

[9]These actions are described in the three Synoptic Gospels and are later repeated by Jesus during the Last Supper.

[10]Jn 6:27.

[11]Jn 6:54.

[12]Joel 2:24.

[13]Rolland and Heidi Baker, *Always Enough: God's Miraculous Provision Among the Poorest Children on Earth* (Chosen Books, 2002), 49.

[14]Jn 12:24.

8. HOSPITALITY

[1]Lk 15:31.

[2]Henri Nouwen, *The Return of the Prodigal Son*, (DoubleDay, 1992), 108-9.

[3]Rom 8:17.

[4]Nouwen, *Return of the Prodigal Son,* 119.

[5]Ed Smither, *Mission as Hospitality: Imitating the Hospitable God in Mission* (Cascade Books, 2021), chap. 6, Kindle.

[6]Is 25:6-8.

[7]Miroslav Volf, *Free of Charge: Giving and Receiving in a Culture Stripped of Grace* (Zondervan, 2005), chap. 1, Kindle.

[8]Volf, *Free of Charge*, chap. 1, Kindle.

[9]Christine Pohl, *Making Room: Recovering Hospitality as a Christian Tradition* (Eerdmans, 1990), 16-17.

[10]Raghu Rai and Navin Chawla, *Faith and Compassion: The Life and Work of Mother Teresa* (Element Books, 1996), 50.

[11]Rom 12:1.

[12]Oswald Chambers, *My Utmost for His Highest* (Discover House, 1992), reading for May 15.

[13]Henri Nouwen, *In the Name of Jesus: Reflections on Christian Leadership* (Crossroad Publishing, 1989), 61.

[14]This is another concept of Henri Nouwen's and the title of his book *The Wounded Healer: Ministry in Contemporary Society* (Doubleday, 1972).

[15]Robert's words, originally a Facebook post on June 19, 2024, were later published as Robert Cunningham, "The Wounds of God for the People of God," *Mockingbird*, July 15, 2024, https://mbird.com/theology/the-wounds-of-god-for-the-people-of-god.

9. COURAGE

[1]Wendell Berry, *A World Lost* (Counterpoint, 1996), 149.

[2]In a Holy Week reflection at Salisbury Cathedral, Sarah Coakley commented on the traditional belief that Judas hanged himself after betraying Jesus: "God can make love, excessive love, even out of human betrayal. On this view Judas's tragedy was that—unlike Peter—he despaired of that possibility; he could not conceive of that excessive sort of forgiveness." Sarah Coakley, "Holy Week at Salisbury Cathedral: Betrayal," March 27, 2013, www.fulcrum-anglican.org.uk/articles/holy-week-at-salisbury-cathedral-betrayal-address-3.

[3]Jn 13:1.

[4]In 1 Corinthians 11:23-26, Paul grounds his instructions for the Lord's Supper in Jesus' words at the Last Supper.

[5]Paul Bradshaw and Maxwell Johnson, *The Eucharistic Liturgies: Their Evolution and Interpretation,* (Liturgical Press, 2012), 123.

[6]Bradshaw and Johnson, *Eucharistic Liturgies*, 129.

[7]Caitlyn Schmid, "On the 34th Anniversary of Oscar Romero's Assassination," *U.S. Catholic*, March 24, 2014, https://uscatholic.org/blog/on-the-34th-anniversary-of-oscar-romeros-assassination.

[8]C. S. Lewis, *The Four Loves* (HarperOne, 1960), chap. 6, Kindle.

[9]Lewis, *Four Loves*, chap. 6, Kindle.

[10]E. Lily Yu, *Break Blow Burn and Make: A Writer's Thoughts on Creation* (Worthy Publishing, 2024), 215.

[11]Lewis, *Four Loves*, chap. 6, Kindle.

10. HOME

[1]Gen 3:8.

[2]Humphrey Carpenter, *The Letters of J. R. R. Tolkien: Revised and Expanded Edition* (HarperCollins, 2023), 159.

[3]Frederick Buechner, *Longing for Home: Recollections and Reflections* (HarperCollins, 1996), part 1 and part 2.

[4]Whitney Woollard, "What Is the Significance of the Promised Land in the Bible? Tracing the Theme Through Four Cycles of Scripture," *The Bible Project*, May 4, 2014, https://bibleproject.com/articles/land-thermometer-covenantal-faithfulness.

[5]Mt 26:29.

[6]A close rendition of Paul's prayer from 1 Corinthians 16:22 is included in the *Didache* (10:6) in a section regarding eucharistic liturgical instruction.

[7]Buechner, *Longing for Home*, 17.

[8]Buechner, *Longing for Home*, 18.

[9]Jer 29:7.

[10]Amy Baik Lee, *This Homeward Ache: How Our Yearning for the Life to Come Spurs on Our Life Today* (B&H Publishing), 91.

[11]Lee, *This Homeward Ache*, 92-93, quoting Anthony Esolen's introduction to *Nostalgia: Going Home in a Homeless World* (Regnery Gateway, 2018).

[12]Ex 3:8.

[13]Ex 16:31.

[14]Brant Pitre, *Jesus and the Jewish Roots of the Eucharist: Unlocking the Secrets of the Last Supper* (Image, 2011), 84.

[15]See Jn 6:32-33.

[16]J. Todd Billings, *Remembrance, Communion, and Hope: Rediscovering the Gospel at the Lord's Table* (Eerdmans, 2018), chap. 1, Kindle.

[17]Rev 21:1-5.

EPILOGUE

[1]See Jn 1:35-39.

[2]Robert Farrar Capon, *The Supper of the Lamb* (Konecky and Konecky, 1967), 188.

[3]Jn 6:51.

[4]Jn 21:15.

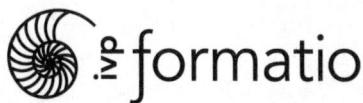

formatio

The nautilus is one of the sea's oldest creatures. Beginning with a tight center, its remarkable growth pattern can be seen in the ever-enlarging chambers that spiral outward. The nautilus in the IVP Formatio logo symbolizes deep inward work of spiritual formation that begins rooted in our souls and then opens to the world as we experience spiritual transformation. The shell takes on a stunning pearlized appearance as it ages and forms in much the same way as the souls of those who devote themselves to spiritual practice. Formatio books draw on the ancient wisdom of the saints and the early church as well as the rich resources of Scripture, applying tradition to the needs of contemporary life and practice.

Within each of us is a longing to be in God's presence. Formatio books call us into our deepest desires and help us to become our true selves in the light of God's grace.

LIKE THIS BOOK?

Scan the code to discover more content like this!

Get on IVP's email list to receive special offers, exclusive book news, and thoughtful content from your favorite authors on topics you care about.

IVPRESS.COM/BOOK-QR

"If your church observes the Lord's Supper infrequently, you may wonder what all the fuss is about. Can eating bread and drinking wine in a worship service really make a difference in one's life with God? In this beautifully written book, Hannah Miller King demonstrates the power of Holy Communion by generously, humbly describing the difference it has made in hers. Profound, mature, instructive, and deeply consoling, this book is a gift for the people of God."

Wesley Hill, associate professor of New Testament at Western Theological Seminary

"In this beautiful meditation, weaving together her experience as an Anglican priest and the pain and hope she's met in her own life, Hannah Miller King helps us understand why the Eucharist has always been central for Christian worship. It is a meal that teaches us to live in the in-between, where joy and sorrow are indissolubly bound together. This is a book that rewards slow and attentive reading and revisiting. Highly recommended!"

Tish Harrison Warren, Anglican priest and author of *Liturgy of the Ordinary* and *Prayer in the Night*

"In Hannah Miller King's fabulous book, *Feasting on Hope*, we are reminded of things that we all-too quickly forget but desperately need to remember. We are reminded that our Lord feeds the hungry with bread that exceeds their deepest hungers, along with their greatest sorrows; satisfies the thirsty with wine that lasts for days; sits the stranger at the head table, not the kid one; sets the penniless and powerless at feasting tables while enemies watch nearby; and makes the wasteland of our lives blossom with beauty that both pierces and gladdens our hearts. Above all, he nourishes our bodies and souls with living food and the blood that is true drink. He does so with his very own self. There's so much to feast on in this book. I say: eat up and enjoy!"

W. David O. Taylor, associate professor of theology and culture at Fuller Theological Seminary and author of *Prayers for the Pilgrimage* and *A Body of Praise*

"Our Father has spread a table in the wilderness for us. His Son Jesus feeds us as we join him at the meal. And the Spirit of God unites us in his love as we eat. Hannah Miller King's apt reminder of these supernatural blessings is a word spoken in season. The Lord's Supper does not eradicate our pain and anxiety. But the communion it provides us with the Lord and one another gives us grace and peace now and bright hope for the day when God will make all things new and fulfill our every longing. Please join God's family as we feast."

Douglas A. Sweeney, dean and professor of divinity at Beeson Divinity School at Samford University

"Writing from a deeply personal space, Hannah Miller King explores the beauty and significance of the Lord's Supper as a place of hope and encounter. She weaves in the profound significance of Jesus' embodiment—and our own—for the Lord's Supper and Christian community. With words of grace and hope, she shows how abundance, hospitality, and courage all flow from this sacrament. In the end, she presents the Lord's Supper as the anticipation of our deep longing to be truly home—the home that awaits us when we at last see the Lord face-to-face. This book is an invitation to the feast of weekly communion as well as the feast of seeing its profound significance for all believers. I warmly recommend this book to all who are hungry and long to be fed."

Dana M. Harris, professor of New Testament at Trinity Evangelical Divinity School

"In *Feasting on Hope*, Hannah Miller King does what few writers attempt: She sets a table in the wilderness and invites us to sit honestly with our unanswered questions, our deferred longings, and our persistent ache for home. With disarming vulnerability and pastoral insight, she reminds us that the eucharistic life is not an escape from sorrow but communion with the Man of Sorrows who is himself our feast and our foretaste of the world made new. This book will feed your faith, steady your groaning heart, and send you back into the wilderness with the certainty that God still spreads a table in the desert."

Stephen D. Wood, archbishop of the Anglican Church in North America and bishop of the diocese of the Carolinas